ACCOUNTING PRINCIPLES

FIFTH CANADIAN EDITION

➔ Jerry J. Weygandt *Ph.D., C.P.A.*
University of Wisconsin—Madison

➔ Donald E. Kieso *Ph.D., C.P.A.*
Northern Illinois University

➔ Paul D. Kimmel *Ph.D., C.P.A.*
University of Wisconsin—Milwaukee

➔ Barbara Trenholm *M.B.A., F.C.A.*
University of New Brunswick—Fredericton

➔ Valerie A. Kinnear *M.Sc. (Bus. Admin.), C.A.*
Mount Royal University

Updated by Cécile Laurin, C.A.
Algonquin College

WILEY

John Wiley & Sons Canada, Ltd

Library and Archives Canada Cataloguing in Publication

Accounting principles, fifth Canadian edition. Payroll accounting supplement / Jerry J. Weygandt ... [et al.].

ISBN 978-0-470-67787-2

1. Wages--Accounting--Textbooks. I. Weygandt, Jerry J.

HF5636.A33 2009a Suppl. 2   657'.742   C2009-906898-2

Production Credits
    Acquisitions Editor: Zoë Craig
    Vice President & Publisher: Veronica Visentin
    Vice President, Publishing Services: Karen Bryan
    Creative Director, Publishing Services: Ian Koo
    Marketing Manager: Aida Krneta
    Editorial Manager: Karen Staudinger
    Developmental Editor: Daleara Jamasji Hirjikaka
    Editorial Assistant: Laura Hwee
    Design & Typesetting: OrangeSprocket Communications
    Cover Design: Natalia Burobina
    Printing & Binding: EPAC Book Services

Printed and bound in the United States
1 2 3 4 5 EPAC 14 13 12 11 10

John Wiley & Sons Canada, Ltd.
6045 Freemont Blvd.
Mississauga, Ontario L5R 4J3
Visit our website at: www.wiley.ca

Payroll Accounting

Almost all companies incur salaries (or wages) and benefits expense. It is often the largest expense incurred by a company and companies must also follow provincial and federal laws on employee compensation.

The first part of this expense, salaries and/or wages expense, includes amounts paid to employees (net pay) and amounts paid by employees (payroll deductions). These are collectively known as **employee payroll costs**.

In addition to paying employee salaries and wages, employers also have to pay employee benefits. Employee benefits result in another type of expense for the employer, known as employee benefits expense. Employee benefits, or **employer payroll costs**, include amounts paid by the employer on behalf of the employee, such as the employer's share of the Canada Pension and Employment Insurance Plans. We will explore employee and employer payroll costs in the following sections.

Employee Payroll Costs

Determining the payroll costs for employees involves calculating (1) gross pay, (2) payroll deductions, and (3) net pay.

Gross Pay

Gross pay, or earnings, is the total compensation earned by an employee. It consists of wages or salaries, plus any bonuses and commissions. While the terms *salaries* and *wages* are often used interchangeably, managerial, administrative, and sales personnel are generally paid salaries. Salaries are often expressed as a specific amount per week, per month, or per year. If the rate is a yearly rate, it is prorated over the number of payroll periods (e.g., 26 biweekly periods, 52 weekly periods, etc.) that the company uses. Most executive and administrative positions are salaried and do not earn overtime pay.

Part-time employees, store clerks, factory employees, and manual labourers are normally paid wages. Total wages for an employee are determined by multiplying the hours worked by the hourly rate of pay. Companies are also required by law to pay hourly workers overtime. The minimum amount that must be paid for overtime will vary by province. For example, in Ontario, employers must pay at least one and one half times ("time and a half") the regular hourly wage for overtime work.

The number of hours that need to be worked before overtime becomes payable is based on a **standard work week**. The standard work week will vary by industry, occupation, and province. For example, in Ontario, the standard work week is 44 hours and an employer must pay overtime for every hour worked over 44 hours per week. On the other hand, in British Columbia and Manitoba, most employees who work more than 40 hours per week are entitled to overtime. An employer should always review the appropriate employment standards legislation for their own jurisdiction when calculating gross pay.

Note that salaries and wages do not include payments made for the services of professionals outside the company such as accountants, lawyers, and architects. Such professionals are independent contractors rather than salaried employees. Payments to them are called fees, rather than salaries or wages. This distinction is important, because government regulations for the payment and reporting of payroll apply only to employees.

To illustrate the calculation of gross pay, assume that Mark Jordan works for Academy Company, in Toronto, Ontario, as a shipping clerk. His regular pay rate is $20 per hour. The calculation of Mark's gross pay (total wages) for the 48 hours shown on his time card for the weekly pay period ending June 20, 2009, is as follows:

Type of Pay	Hours	×	Rate	=	Gross Pay
Regular	44	×	$20	=	$ 880
Overtime	4	×	$30	=	120
Total wages					$1,000

This calculation assumes that Mark Jordan receives one and one-half times his regular hourly rate ($20 × 1.5) for any hours worked in excess of 44 hours per week (overtime).

Payroll Deductions

As anyone who has received a paycheque knows, gross pay is usually very different from the amount that is actually received. The difference is due to **payroll deductions**. Payroll deductions are also frequently called "withholdings" because these are the amounts that the employer withholds, or holds back, from the employee.

Payroll deductions do not result in an expense for the employer. The employer is only a collection agent. The amounts withheld from the employee are later paid to the government (for deductions such as income tax, CPP, and EI) or to some other agency (for deductions such as a union, an insurance company, or the United Way). The designated collection agency for the federal government is the Canada Revenue Agency (CRA), which collects money on behalf of the Receiver General for Canada, the cabinet minister responsible for accepting payments to the Government of Canada.

Payroll deductions may be mandatory or voluntary. Illustration P-1 summarizes the types of payroll deductions that most companies usually make.

Illustration P-1 ➡

Employee payroll deductions

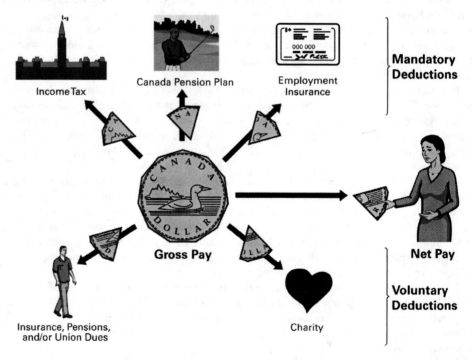

Mandatory Payroll Deductions. Mandatory deductions are required by law and include personal income tax, Canada Pension Plan contributions, and Employment Insurance premiums. We will discuss these three deductions in the following sections.

Canada Pension Plan (CPP). All employees 18 and older, but younger than 70 (except those employed in the province of Quebec), must contribute to the **Canada Pension Plan**. Quebec has its own similar program, the Quebec Pension Plan (QPP). These plans give extra disability, retirement, and death benefits to qualifying Canadians.

Each year, based on changes in the cost of living, the federal government sets the maximum pensionable earnings, the basic yearly exemption, and the contribution rates that are used when calculating the CPP contributions to deduct from employees. As of January 1, 2009, the following amounts were in effect:

Maximum pensionable earnings	$46,300
Basic yearly exemption	$3,500
CPP contribution rate	4.95%
Maximum annual employee CPP contribution	$2,118.60

Pensionable earnings are gross earnings less the basic yearly exemption.
The required CPP contribution for each pay period is calculated by following these steps:

1. Calculate the basic pay-period exemption to be applied. To do this, divide the basic yearly exemption by the number of pay periods in a year. For example, if employees are paid weekly, divide the basic yearly exemption by 52.
2. Calculate the employee's pensionable earnings by subtracting the result of step 1 from the employee's gross pay in the period.
3. Calculate the CPP contribution by multiplying the result of step 2 by the CPP contribution rate.

Illustration P-2 shows the formulas and calculations used to determine Mark Jordan's CPP contribution on his gross pay of $1,000 for the weekly pay period ending June 20, 2009.

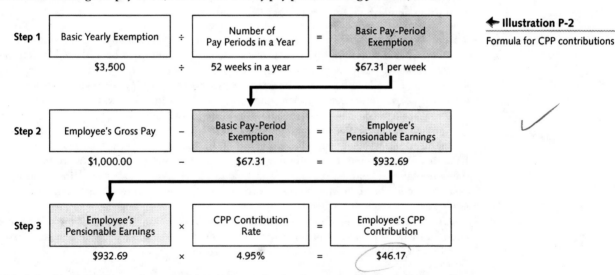

◀ **Illustration P-2**

Formula for CPP contributions

Mark Jordan's CPP contribution of $21.42 can also be determined by using a payroll accounting program or one of several payroll deduction calculation tools available from the CRA. We will discuss the CRA payroll deduction calculation tools in a later section.

An employer stops deducting CPP contributions if and when the employee's earnings are greater than the maximum pensionable earnings. By doing this the employee's CPP contributions will not be greater than the maximum CPP an employee is required to contribute in a year. Self-employed individuals pay both the employee and employer share of CPP.

Employment Insurance (EI). The *Employment Insurance Act* requires all Canadian workers, who are not self-employed, to pay Employment Insurance (EI) premiums. **Employment Insurance** is designed to give income protection for a limited period of time to employees who are temporarily laid off, who are on parental leave, or who lose their jobs.

Each year, the federal government determines the maximum annual insurable earnings and the contribution rate that employers use when calculating the EI premiums to deduct from employees. Different from CPP, there is no basic yearly exemption. For 2009, the following amounts were in effect:

Maximum insurable earnings	$42,300
EI contribution rate	1.73%
Maximum annual employee EI premium	$731.79

In most cases, **insurable earnings** are gross earnings.

The required EI premium is calculated by multiplying the employee's insurable earnings by the EI contribution rate. Illustration P-3 shows the formula and calculations to determine Mark Jordan's EI premium on his gross pay of $1,000 for the pay period ending June 20.

Illustration P-3 ➡

Formula for EI premiums

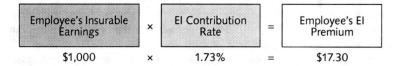

Employee's Insurable Earnings	×	EI Contribution Rate	=	Employee's EI Premium
$1,000	×	1.73%	=	$17.30

Mark Jordan's EI premium of $17.30 can also be determined by using a payroll accounting program or one of several other payroll deduction calculation tools available from the CRA. We will discuss the CRA payroll deduction calculation tools in the next section. An employer stops deducting EI premiums if and when the employee's earnings are greater than the maximum insurable earnings. By doing this the employee's EI premiums will not be greater than the maximum EI an employee is required to pay in a year.

Personal Income Tax. In accordance with the *Income Tax Act*, employers are required to withhold income tax from employees each pay period. The amount to be withheld is determined by three variables: (1) the employee's gross pay, (2) the personal tax credits claimed by the employee, and (3) the length of the pay period. **Personal tax credits** are amounts deducted from an individual's income taxes and determine the amount of income taxes to be withheld.

Every resident of Canada can claim a basic personal amount as a personal tax credit on their personal income tax return. Therefore, when an employer is calculating the amount of income tax to be withheld from its employees' gross pay, the employer makes an allowance for the basic personal amount. In addition, an employee may request an adjustment to the amount of income tax withheld if they know in advance that they will be able to claim additional personal tax credits on their income tax return. To do this the employee must complete a federal Personal Tax Credits Return or TD1 form.

On the TD1 form, the employee calculates the total amount of personal income tax credits based on their best estimate of their circumstances. Some of the personal tax credits listed on the federal **TD1** form—amounts based on the rates in effect in 2009—include:

4. Basic personal amount $10,375
5. Spouse or common-law amount   10,375
6. Disability amount   7,196

Basically, the purpose of the TD1 form is to give employees—who have legitimate circumstances—a choice about whether they receive a larger paycheque during the year or receive an annual income tax refund after the employee has filed their personal income tax return. It is important to emphasize that employees are only allowed to request a reduction to income tax withholdings in legitimate circumstances as outlined on the form. The CRA includes a warning on the TD1 form that it is a serious offence to make a false return.

The TD1 form can also be used by the employee to tell their employer to increase the income taxes withheld each paycheque. Employees may choose to do this if they know in advance they will have to pay additional income taxes when filing their personal income tax return, and they wish to avoid having to make a single larger payment.

The employee must complete a new TD1 each time there is a change in their circumstances. If an employee has not completed the TD1, the employer uses only the basic personal amount when calculating income taxes.

Helpful hint TD1 forms are available for downloading on the CRA's website: http://www.cra-arc.gc.ca/formspubs/frms/td1-eng.html

It is also important to note that employees who claim more than the basic personal amount also have to complete the TD1 that corresponds to their province or territory of employment. Each province has different amounts for the personal tax credits. For example, in 2009, the basic personal amount on the Ontario Personal Tax Credits Return (TD1ON) is $8,881.

As mentioned above, income tax deductions are also based on an employee's gross pay. There is no limit on the amount of gross pay that is subject to income tax withholdings. In addition, the federal government, and all of the provincial governments except Alberta, use a progressive tax scheme when calculating income taxes. Basically, this means that the higher the pay or earnings, the higher the income tax percentage, and thus the higher the amount of taxes withheld. For example, in 2009, the federal tax rates were:

- 15.0% on the first $41,200 of taxable income, +
- 22% on the next $41,199 of taxable income (on the portion of taxable income between $41,200.01 and $82,399), +
- 26% on the next $43,865 of taxable income (on the portion of taxable income between $82,399.01 and $126,264), +
- 29% of taxable income over $126,264.01.

As you can see, the calculation of personal income tax withholdings is complicated. Consequently, it is best done using one of the many payroll accounting programs that are available or by using the payroll deduction tools supplied by the CRA. We will discuss the payroll deduction tools available from the CRA in a later section. For now, assume that we have determined the total income tax owed for Mark Jordan using the CRA tables. His federal income tax is $124.70 and his provincial income tax is $67.25, for a total income tax owed of $191.95 on his gross pay of $1,000.

Helpful hint Examples of some of the more common payroll accounting programs used by small business include Simply Accounting, QuickBooks Payroll, and Peachtree Accounting.

Determining Mandatory Payroll Deductions. As mentioned earlier, there are several methods employers can use to determine the correct payroll deductions. Companies may choose to use a payroll accounting program, or one of the payroll deduction tools available from the CRA. In this section we will discuss three of the methods available from the CRA: (1) Payroll Deduction Tables, (2) Tables on Diskette (TOD), and (3) Payroll Deductions Online Calculator (PDOC).

Payroll Deduction Tables. **Payroll deduction tables** are prepared by the CRA and can be easily downloaded from the CRA website at <http://www.cra-arc.gc.ca/tx/bsnss/tpcs/pyrll/menu-eng.html>. There are separate payroll deduction tables for determining federal tax deductions, provincial tax deductions, Canada Pension Plan contributions, and Employment Insurance premiums.

These tables are updated at least once a year on January 1 to reflect the new rates for that year. Income tax tables are also reissued during the year if the federal or provincial governments make changes to income tax rates during the year. It is important to make sure you have the tables that are in effect during the payroll period for which you are calculating deductions.

There are separate sections of the federal and provincial income tax and the CPP tables for weekly, biweekly, semimonthly, and monthly pay periods. Thus, when determining these amounts it is important to make sure you are using the table prepared for the company's pay period. The Academy Company would use the weekly tables.

Federal Tax Deduction Tables. There are five steps to locating the correct deduction in the federal tax deduction tables. Illustration P-4, on the next page, is an excerpt from the federal tax tables and shows how Academy Company follows the steps described below to determine Mark Jordan's federal tax deduction of $124.70 as given in an earlier section.

Step 1: Obtain the federal income tax tables in effect for the pay period. The tables are updated at the beginning of each year and sometimes at July 1, because of changes in income tax rates. For the pay period ending June 20, 2009, Academy Company would use the tables effective April 1, 2009.

Step 2: Select the section of the tables that corresponds with the company's pay period. There are different tables for weekly, biweekly, semi-monthly, and monthly pay periods. Academy Company has a weekly pay period and will use the weekly tables.

Step 3: Locate the employee's gross pay for the pay period in the first column of the table. The first column shows pay ranges listed in increasing amounts. Mark Jordan's gross pay for the pay period ending June 20, 2009, was $1,000. In Illustration P-4 we can see that $1,000 falls in the range "from $1,000 to less than $1,012." If Mark's gross pay had been $1,015, we would use the next range on the table.

Step 4: Determine the correct Federal Claim Code. The claim codes are based on the total personal tax credits claimed in the TD1 return discussed in a previous section. The employer must match the total claim amount in the TD1 with the claim codes according to a chart included with the Payroll Tax Tables. Claim Code "0" is used for non-residents of Canada who cannot claim the basic personal amount. Claim Code "1" is used for employees who are claiming only the basic personal amount. The chart also shows how to convert the amount of personal tax credits into Claim Codes "2" to "10." We will assume that Claim Code 1 is the correct code for Mark Jordan.

Step 5: Find the federal tax deduction by looking for the number in the correct gross earnings row and in the correct claim code column.

Illustration P-4

Excerpt from Federal Tax Deduction Tables

Step 1 | Step 2 | Step 3 | Step 4 | Step 5

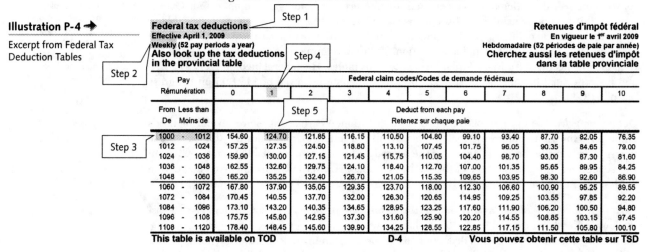

Federal tax deductions
Effective April 1, 2009
Weekly (52 pay periods a year)
Also look up the tax deductions in the provincial table

Retenues d'impôt fédéral
En vigueur le 1er avril 2009
Hebdomadaire (52 périodes de paie par année)
Cherchez aussi les retenues d'impôt dans la table provinciale

Pay / Rémunération	Federal claim codes/Codes de demande fédéraux										
	0	1	2	3	4	5	6	7	8	9	10
From Less than / De Moins de	Deduct from each pay / Retenez sur chaque paie										
1000 - 1012	154.60	124.70	121.85	116.15	110.50	104.80	99.10	93.40	87.70	82.05	76.35
1012 - 1024	157.25	127.35	124.50	118.80	113.10	107.45	101.75	96.05	90.35	84.65	79.00
1024 - 1036	159.90	130.00	127.15	121.45	115.75	110.05	104.40	98.70	93.00	87.30	81.60
1036 - 1048	162.55	132.60	129.75	124.10	118.40	112.70	107.00	101.35	95.65	89.95	84.25
1048 - 1060	165.20	135.25	132.40	126.70	121.05	115.35	109.65	103.95	98.30	92.60	86.90
1060 - 1072	167.80	137.90	135.05	129.35	123.70	118.00	112.30	106.60	100.90	95.25	89.55
1072 - 1084	170.45	140.55	137.70	132.00	126.30	120.65	114.95	109.25	103.55	97.85	92.20
1084 - 1096	173.10	143.20	140.35	134.65	128.95	123.25	117.60	111.90	106.20	100.50	94.80
1096 - 1108	175.75	145.80	142.95	137.30	131.60	125.90	120.20	114.55	108.85	103.15	97.45
1108 - 1120	178.40	148.45	145.60	139.90	134.25	128.55	122.85	117.15	111.50	105.80	100.10

This table is available on TOD D-4 **Vous pouvez obtenir cette table sur TSD**

In Illustration P-4 we can see that the intersection of the pay range from the $1,000 to $1,012 row and the Claim Code 1 column is $124.70.

Provincial Tax Deduction Tables. The steps involved in determining the correct deduction in the provincial tax deduction are similar to those used with the federal tax deduction tables. Illustration P-5, on the following page, is an excerpt from the Ontario provincial tax tables and shows how Academy Company follows the steps described below to determine Mark Jordan's provincial tax deduction of $67.25 as given in an earlier section.

Step 1: Obtain the provincial tables in effect for the pay period. Provincial tables, similar to federal tables, are updated regularly. For the pay period ending June 20, 2009, Academy Company would use the Ontario tables effective April 1, 2009.

Step 2: Select the section of the tables that corresponds with the company's pay period—Academy Company will use the weekly tables.

Step 3: Locate the employee's gross pay for the pay period in the first column of the table. The first column shows pay ranges listed in increasing amounts. In Illustration P-5 we can see that Mark Jordan's gross pay of $1,000 falls in the range "from $994 to less than $1,002."

Step 4:   Determine the correct Provincial Claim Code. Provincial Claim Codes are similar to Federal Claim Codes. The only difference between the two is that there is a different chart for provincial claim codes, with different amounts, in the payroll tables. An employer should not automatically assume an employee will have the same federal and provincial claim codes. We will assume that Claim Code 1 is the correct code for Mark Jordan.

Step 5:   Find the provincial tax deduction by looking for the number in the correct gross earnings row and in the correct claim code column.

Illustration P-5

Excerpt from Ontario Provincial Tax Deduction Tables

Ontario provincial tax deductions
Effective April 1, 2009
Weekly (52 pay periods a year)
Also look up the tax deductions in the federal table

Retenues d'impôt provincial de l'Ontario
En vigueur le 1er avril 2009
Hebdomadaire (52 périodes de paie par année)
Cherchez aussi les retenues d'impôt dans la table fédérale

Pay Rémunération		Provincial claim codes/Codes de demande provinciaux										
		0	1	2	3	4	5	6	7	8	9	10
From De	Less than Moins de					Deduct from each pay / Retenez sur chaque paie						
938	946	72.45	62.10	61.00	58.80	56.55	54.35	52.10	49.90	47.65	45.45	43.20
946	954	73.20	62.85	61.75	59.50	57.30	55.05	52.85	50.60	48.40	46.15	43.95
954	962	73.90	63.60	62.45	60.25	58.00	55.80	53.55	51.35	49.10	46.90	44.65
962	970	74.65	64.30	63.20	61.00	58.75	56.55	54.30	52.10	49.85	47.60	45.40
970	978	75.40	65.05	63.95	61.70	59.50	57.25	55.05	52.80	50.60	48.35	46.15
978	986	76.10	65.80	64.65	62.45	60.20	58.00	55.75	53.55	51.30	49.10	46.85
986	994	76.85	66.50	65.40	63.15	60.95	58.70	56.50	54.25	52.05	49.80	47.60
994	1002	77.60	67.25	66.15	63.90	61.70	59.45	57.25	55.00	52.80	50.55	48.35
1002	1010	78.30	68.00	66.85	64.65	62.40	60.20	57.95	55.75	53.50	51.30	49.05
1010	1018	79.05	68.70	67.60	65.35	63.15	60.90	58.70	56.45	54.25	52.00	49.80

This table is available on TOD   E-3   Vous pouvez obtenir cette table sur TSD

In Illustration P-5 we can see that the intersection of the pay range from the $994 to $1,002 row and the Claim Code 1 column is $67.25.

CPP Contribution Tables. Tables are also available for determining CPP contributions. Illustration P-6 below is an excerpt from the CPP tables and shows how Academy Company can use the tables to determine Mark Jordan's CPP contribution of $45.94 as calculated in an earlier section.

Step 1:   Obtain the Canada Pension Plan contribution tables in effect for the pay period—in this case for 2009.

Step 2:   Select the section of the tables that corresponds with the company's pay period—Academy Company will use the weekly tables.

Step 3:   Locate the employee's gross pay for the pay period—the CPP contribution is in the column to the right of the pay range.

Illustration P-6

Excerpt from CPP Contribution Tables

Canada Pension Plan Contributions
Weekly (52 pay periods a year)

Cotisations au Régime de pensions du Canada
Hebdomadaire (52 périodes de paie par année)

Pay Rémunération		CPP RPC	Pay Rémunération		CPP RPC	Pay Rémunération		CPP RPC	Pay Rémunération		CPP RPC
From - De	To - À		From - De	To - À		From - De	To - À		From - De	To - À	
910.44	920.43	41.98	1630.44	1640.43	77.62	2350.44	2360.43	113.26	3070.44	3080.43	148.90
920.44	930.43	42.48	1640.44	1650.43	78.12	2360.44	2370.43	113.76	3080.44	3090.43	149.40
930.44	940.43	42.97	1650.44	1660.43	78.61	2370.44	2380.43	114.25	3090.44	3100.43	149.89
940.44	950.43	43.47	1660.44	1670.43	79.11	2380.44	2390.43	114.75	3100.44	3110.43	150.39
950.44	960.43	43.96	1670.44	1680.43	79.60	2390.44	2400.43	115.24	3110.44	3120.43	150.88
960.44	970.43	44.46	1680.44	1690.43	80.10	2400.44	2410.43	115.74	3120.44	3130.43	151.38
970.44	980.43	44.95	1690.44	1700.43	80.59	2410.44	2420.43	116.23	3130.44	3140.43	151.87
980.44	990.43	45.45	1700.44	1710.43	81.09	2420.44	2430.43	116.73	3140.44	3150.43	152.37
990.44	1000.43	45.94	1710.44	1720.43	81.58	2430.44	2440.43	117.22	3150.44	3160.43	152.86
1000.44	1010.43	46.44	1720.44	1730.43	82.08	2440.44	2450.43	117.72	3160.44	3170.43	153.36
1010.44	1020.43	46.93	1730.44	1740.43	82.57	2450.44	2460.43	118.21	3170.44	3180.43	153.85
1020.44	1030.43	47.43	1740.44	1750.43	83.07	2460.44	2470.43	118.71	3180.44	3190.43	154.35
1030.44	1040.43	47.92	1750.44	1760.43	83.56	2470.44	2480.43	119.20	3190.44	3200.43	154.84
1040.44	1050.43	48.42	1760.44	1770.43	84.06	2480.44	2490.43	119.70	3200.44	3210.43	155.34
1050.44	1060.43	48.91	1770.44	1780.43	84.55	2490.44	2500.43	120.19	3210.44	3220.43	155.83
1060.44	1070.43	49.41	1780.44	1790.43	85.05	2500.44	2510.43	120.69	3220.44	3230.43	156.33
1070.44	1080.43	49.90	1790.44	1800.43	85.54	2510.44	2520.43	121.18	3230.44	3240.43	156.82
1080.44	1090.43	50.40	1800.44	1810.43	86.04	2520.44	2530.43	121.68	3240.44	3250.43	157.32

Employee's maximum CPP contribution for the year 2009 is $2,118.60   B-15   La cotisation maximale de l'employé au RPC pour l'année 2009 est de 2 118,60 $

In Illustration P-6 we can see that Mark Jordan's gross pay of $1,000 falls in the range "from $990.44 to $1,000.43." The required CPP contribution of $45.94 is recorded in the column to the right of this range.

EI Premium Tables. Employers may use tables to determine EI premiums. Illustration P-7 is an excerpt from the EI tables and shows how Academy Company can determine Mark Jordan's EI premium of $17.30 as calculated in an earlier section.

Step 1: Obtain the Employment Insurance premium tables in effect for the pay period—in this case for 2009.

Step 2: Locate the employee's gross pay in the table—the EI premium is in the column to the right of the pay range.

Illustration P-7 →

Excerpt from EI Premium Tables

Employment Insurance Premiums   Step 1   **Cotisations à l'assurance-emploi**

Insurable Earnings Rémunération assurable		EI premium Cotisation d'AE	Insurable Earnings Rémunération assurable		EI premium Cotisation d'AE	Insurable Earnings Rémunération assurable		EI premium Cotisation d'AE	Insurable Earnings Rémunération assurable		EI premium Cotisation d'AE
From - De	To - À		From - De	To - À		From - De	To - À		From - De	To - À	
999.14 -	999.71	17.29	1040.76 -	1041.32	18.01	1082.37 -	1082.94	18.73	1123.99 -	1124.56	19.45
999.72 -	1000.28	17.30	1041.33 -	1041.90	18.02	1082.95 -	1083.52	18.74	1124.57 -	1125.14	19.46
1000.29 -	1000.86	17.31	1041.91 -	1042.48	18.03	1083.53 -	1084.10	18.75	1125.15 -	1125.72	19.47
1000.87 -	1001.44	17.32	1042.49 -	1043.06	18.04	1084.11 -	1084.68	18.76	1125.73 -	1126.30	19.48
1001.45 -	1002.02	17.33	1043.07 -	1043.64	18.05	1084.69 -	1085.26	18.77	1126.31 -	1126.87	19.49
1002.03 -	1002.60	17.34	1043.65 -	1044.21	18.06	1085.27 -	1085.83	18.78	1126.88 -	1127.45	19.50
1002.61 -	1003.17	17.35	1044.22 -	1044.79	18.07	1085.84 -	1086.41	18.79	1127.46 -	1128.03	19.51
1003.18 -	1003.75	17.36	1044.80 -	1045.37	18.08	1086.42 -	1086.99	18.80	1128.04 -	1128.61	19.52
1003.76 -	1004.33	17.37	1045.38 -	1045.95	18.09	1087.00 -	1087.57	18.81	1128.62 -	1129.19	19.53
1004.34 -	1004.91	17.38	1045.96 -	1046.53	18.10	1087.58 -	1088.15	18.82	1129.20 -	1129.76	19.54
1004.92 -	1005.49	17.39	1046.54 -	1047.10	18.11	1088.16 -	1088.72	18.83	1129.77 -	1130.34	19.55
1005.50 -	1006.06	17.40	1047.11 -	1047.68	18.12	1088.73 -	1089.30	18.84	1130.35 -	1130.92	19.56
1006.07 -	1006.64	17.41	1047.69 -	1048.26	18.13	1089.31 -	1089.88	18.85	1130.93 -	1131.50	19.57
1006.65 -	1007.22	17.42	1048.27 -	1048.84	18.14	1089.89 -	1090.46	18.86	1131.51 -	1132.08	19.58

Step 2

Yearly maximum insurable earnings are $42,300
Yearly maximum employee premiums are $731.79
The premium rate for 2009 is 1.73 %

C-7

Le maximum annuel de la rémunération assurable est de 42 300 $
La cotisation maximale annuelle de l'employé est de 731,79 $
Le taux de cotisation pour 2009 est de 1,73 %

In Illustration P-7 we can see that Mark Jordan's gross pay of $1,000 falls in the range "from $999.72 to $1,000.28." The required EI premium of $17.30 is recorded in the column to the right of this range.

Tables on Diskette (TOD). Instead of looking up the appropriate deduction in four different tables, an employer may simply download the file "Tables on Diskette" from the CRA's website <http://www.cra-arc.gc.ca/tx/bsnss/tod-tsd/menu-eng.html>. Similar to the payroll deduction tables, this program is updated by the CRA at least annually and sometimes at July 1 as well. Employers must make sure they are using the correct version TOD.

When using this program, the employer specifies the appropriate province, pay period, gross salary, and claim codes. The program then performs the lookup function and accurately calculates payroll information.

Illustration P-8, on the following page, shows the TOD results for Mark Jordan's payroll. For a weekly wage of $1,000, with an assumed TD1 claim code of 1, the federal and Ontario income taxes to be withheld total $191.95. CPP and EI contributions are $46.17 and $17.30, respectively.

✦ Canada Revenue Agency	Agence du revenu du Canada	

Tables On Diskette

Printed on: 9/15/09

Payroll Deductions for Salary - Effective April 1, 2009 - TOD 1.10

Employee's name (optional)	Mark Jordan		
Employer's name (optional)	Academy Company		
Pay Period ending date (optional)	2009-06-20		
Gross salary (or pension income) for the pay period			1000.00
Total EI insurable earnings for the pay period			1000.00
Taxable salary or pension income			1000.00
Federal tax deductions	124.70		
Provincial or territorial tax deductions	67.25		
Total tax on salary or pension income	191.95	191.95	
Canada Pension Plan (CPP) deductions		46.17	
Employment Insurance (EI) deductions		17.30	
Requested additional tax deduction		0.00	
Total deductions on salary or pension income		255.42	255.42
Net amount			744.58
Total claim amount (from federal TD1)	Claim Code 1 (Minimum - 10,375.00)		
Total claim amount (from provincial or territorial TD1)	Claim Code 1 (Minimum - 8,881.00)		
Pay period	Weekly (52 pay periods a year)		
Province or territory of employment	Ontario		

✦ Illustration P-8

TOD—Tables on Diskette Payroll Deductions

Payroll Deduction Online Calculator (PDOC). Instead of downloading the TOD program, an employer may simply use the on-line deduction calculator available on the CRA's website <http://www.cra-arc.gc.ca/esrvc-srvce/tx/bsnss/pdoc-eng.html>. Similar to TOD, an employer will specify the appropriate province, pay period, gross salary, and claim codes; the PDOC then calculates the payroll deductions. One of the benefits of the PDOC is that it is automatically updated for any changes in rates. As previously mentioned, if an employer is using the TOD program or the payroll deduction tables, they will need to obtain an updated version at least once and frequently twice a year. Illustration P-9 below, shows the PDOC results for Mark Jordan's payroll.

✦ Canada Revenue Agency Agence du revenu du Canada	**Canada**

Payroll Deductions Online Calculator

Results - Effective April 1, 2009

Employee's name	Mark Jordan
Employer's name	Academy Company
Pay period	Weekly (52 pay periods a year)
Pay period ending date	2009-06-20
Province of employment	Ontario
Federal amount from TD1	Claim Code 1 (Minimum - 10,375.00)
Provincial amount from TD1	Claim Code 1 (Minimum - 8,881.00)
Salary or wages for the pay period	1,000.00
Total EI insurable earnings for the pay period	1,000.00
Taxable income	1,000.00
Cash income for the pay period	1,000.00
Federal tax deductions	123.38
Provincial tax deductions	67.43
Requested additional tax deduction	0.00
Total tax on income	190.81
CPP deductions	46.17
EI deductions	17.30
Amounts deducted at source	0.00
Total deductions on income	254.28
Net amount	745.72

✦ Illustration P-9

PDOC—Payroll Deductions Online Calculator

The deductions calculated by the PDOC are slightly different than the amounts calculated by TOD or determined from the payroll deduction tables. For example, in Illustration P-9 provincial income taxes are $67.43 as opposed to $67.25 as shown in Illustrations P-5 and P-8. This is because the TOD and the payroll deduction tables use the mid-point of the salary range to determine the tax deductions. The PDOC uses the exact salary to calculate the tax deduction. The CRA states that results from all three methods are correct, but that the PDOC tax deductions are more precise.

Voluntary Payroll Deductions. Unlike mandatory payroll deductions, which are required by law, voluntary payroll deductions are chosen by the employee.

Employees may choose to authorize withholdings for charitable, retirement, and other purposes. All voluntary deductions from gross pay should be authorized in writing by the employee. The authorization may be made individually or as part of a group plan. Deductions for charitable organizations such as the United Way, or for financial arrangements such as Canada Savings Bonds and the repayment of loans from company credit unions, are made individually. In contrast, deductions for union dues, extended health insurance, life insurance, and pension plans are often made on a group basis. In the calculation of net pay in the next section, we assume that Mark Jordan has a voluntary deduction of $10 for the United Way, and $5 for union dues.

Net Pay

The difference between an employee's gross pay, or total earnings, less any employee payroll deductions withheld from the earnings is known as **net pay**. This is the amount that the employer must pay to the employee. Assuming Academy Company uses payroll deduction tables to calculate mandatory deductions, the net pay for Mark Jordan, for the weekly pay period ending June 20, is $729.81, calculated as follows:

Gross pay		$1,000.00
Payroll deductions:		
Income tax	$191.95	
CPP	45.94	
EI	17.30	
United Way	10.00	
Union dues	5.00	270.19
Net pay		$ 729.81

Before we learn how to record employee payroll costs and deductions, we will turn our attention to *employer* payroll costs. After this discussion, we will record the total employee and employer payroll costs for Academy Company, where Mark Jordan works.

Employer Payroll Costs

Employer payroll costs are amounts that the federal and provincial governments require employers to pay. The federal government requires CPP and EI contributions from employers. The provincial governments require employers to fund a workplace health, safety, and compensation plan. These contributions, plus such items as paid vacations and pensions, are referred to as **employee benefits**.

Canada Pension Plan

We have seen that each employee must contribute to the Canada Pension Plan. The employer must also contribute to the CPP, by matching each employee's contribution. This matching contribution is an employee benefits expense for the employer and is charged at the same rate and according to the same maximum earnings that apply to the employee. Note that employer payroll costs are not debited to the Salaries and Wages Expense account, but rather to a separate Employee Benefits Expense account. The account CPP Payable is used for both the employee's and the employer's CPP contributions. Self-employed individuals must make both the employee's and the employer's contributions. In 2009, the CPP contribution rate for self-employed individuals was 9.90% (4.95% × 2).

Employment Insurance

Employers are required to contribute 1.4 times an employee's EI deductions in a calendar year. The account Employee Benefits Expense is debited for this contribution and EI Payable is credited to recognize this liability. Self-employed individuals do not pay employment insurance premiums and therefore cannot collect employment insurance.

Workplace Health, Safety, and Compensation

The workplace health, safety, and compensation plan gives benefits to workers who are injured or disabled on the job. The cost of this program is paid entirely by the employer; the employee is not required to make contributions to this plan. Employers are assessed a rate—usually between 0.25% and 10% of their gross payroll—based on the risk of injury to employees and past experience.

Helpful hint CPP and EI premiums are paid by both the employer and the employee. Workers' compensation is paid entirely by the employer.

Additional Employee Benefits

In addition to the three employer payroll costs described above, employers have other employee benefit costs. Two of the most important are paid absences and post-employment benefits. We will describe these briefly here, but leave further detail to an intermediate accounting course.

Paid Absences. Employees have the right to receive compensation for absences under certain conditions. The compensation may be for paid vacations, sick pay benefits, and paid statutory holidays. A liability should be estimated and accrued for future paid absences. When the amount cannot be estimated, the potential liability should be disclosed. Ordinarily, vacation pay is the only paid absence that is accrued. Other types of paid absences are only disclosed in notes to the statements.

Post-Employment Benefits. Post-employment benefits are payments by employers to retired or terminated employees. These payments are for (1) supplemental health care, dental care, and life insurance, and (2) pensions. Employers must use the accrual basis in accounting for post-employment benefits. It is important to match the cost of these benefits with the periods where the employer benefits from the services of the employee.

 ## ACCOUNTING IN ACTION: ALL ABOUT YOU

Employers are required by law each month to remit to the CRA mandatory payroll deductions as well as the employer's share of CPP and EI. Failure to do so can lead to interest and stiff penalties.

What happens if you are self-employed and providing consulting services to a company? If you are self-employed, you are required to pay CPP equal to both the employee's and employer's share, and you are also responsible for paying income tax. Starting January 2010, if you are self-employed you can choose to pay EI to qualify for special benefits such as maternity or parental benefits. But this will not qualify you for employment insurance if you are not able to work. If you choose to pay EI, you will not be required to pay the employer's portion of the EI premium.

It may seem beneficial to some companies to hire consultants and avoid paying the employer's share of CPP and EI as well as other benefits. However, the CRA has strict guidelines as to whether an individual is considered an employee or a self-employed consultant. If a company inappropriately treats an individual as self-employed and fails to deduct CPP and EI, the company will be required to pay both the employer's and employee's share of CPP and EI as well as penalties and interest.

If you are providing services to a company, what are the financial advantages and disadvantages of being a self-employed consultant versus an employee of the company?

Recording the Payroll

Recording the payroll involves maintaining payroll records, recording payroll expenses and liabilities, paying the payroll, and filing and remitting payroll deductions.

Payroll Records

Employers are required by law to have payroll records for each employee, and must give each employee a Statement of Remuneration Paid (T4 slip) following the end of each calendar year. The employee then uses it to prepare his or her personal income tax return. This statement shows the employee's employment income and income tax, CPP contributions, and EI premiums deducted for the year, in addition to other voluntary deductions. Although the business issuing the T4 may have a fiscal year end other than a calendar year, T4s must be issued on a calendar year basis. An example of a T4 form for Mark Jordan for 2009, using assumed data, is shown in Illustration P-10.

Illustration P-10 ➡

2009 T4 form

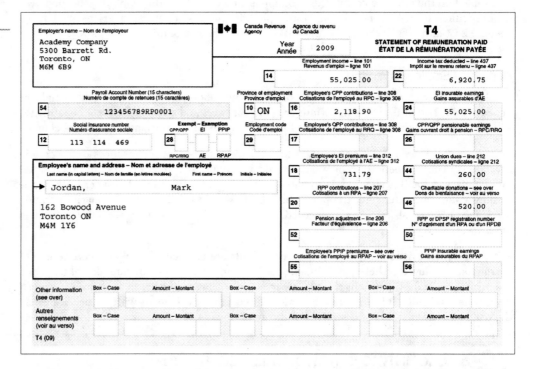

The record that gives this information and other essential data is called the **employee earnings record**. An extract from Mark Jordan's employee earnings record for the month of June is shown in Illustration P-11. This record includes the pay details calculated in Illustration P-8 for the week ending June 20, highlighted in bold text.

ACADEMY COMPANY
Employee Earnings Record
Year Ending December 31, 2009

Name	Mark Jordan	Address	162 Bowood Avenue
Social Insurance Number	113-114-496		Toronto
Date of Birth	December 24, 1985		Ontario, M4N 1Y6
Date Employed	September 1, 2007	Telephone	416-486-0669
Date Employment Ended		E-mail	jordan@sympatico.ca
Job Title	Shipping Clerk	Claim Code	1

2009 Period Ending	Total Hours	Gross Pay				Deductions						Payment	
		Regular	Overtime	Total	Cumulative	CPP	EI	Income Tax	United Way	Union Dues	Total	Net Amount	Cheque #
June 6	46	880.00	60.00	940.00	19,940.00	43.20	16.26	172.30	10.00	5.00	246.76	693.24	974
13	47	880.00	90.00	970.00	20,910.00	44.68	16.78	182.25	10.00	5.00	258.71	711.29	1028
20	**48**	**880.00**	**120.00**	**1,000.00**	**21,910.00**	**46.17**	**17.30**	**191.95**	**10.00**	**5.00**	**270.42**	**729.58**	**1077**
27	46	880.00	60.00	940.00	22,850.00	43.20	16.26	172.30	10.00	5.00	246.76	693.24	1133
June Total		3,520.00	330.00	3,850.00		177.25	66.60	718.80	40.00	20.00	1,022.65	2,827.35	

A separate earnings record is kept for each employee and updated after each pay period. The cumulative payroll data on the earnings record are used by the employer to (1) determine when an employee has reached the maximum earnings subject to CPP and EI premiums, (2) file information returns with the CRA (as explained later in this section), and (3) give each employee a statement of gross pay and withholdings for the year. If an employee is terminated during the year, the employee earnings record information is used to prepare a Record of Employment form (ROE), which the employee then uses to process an employment insurance claim.

In addition to employee earnings records, many companies find it useful to prepare a **payroll register**. This record accumulates the gross pay, deductions, and net pay per employee for each pay period and becomes the documentation for preparing a paycheque for each employee. Academy Company's payroll register is presented in Illustration P-12 below. It shows the data for Mark Jordan in the wages section, highlighted in bold text. In this example, Academy Company's total weekly payroll is $34,420, as shown in the gross pay column.

↑ Illustration P-11

Employee earnings record

↓ Illustration P-12

Payroll register

ACADEMY COMPANY
Payroll Register
Week Ending June 20, 2009

Employee	Total Hours	Gross Pay			Deductions						Payment	
		Regular	Overtime	Gross	CPP	EI	Income Tax	United Way	Union Dues	Total	Net Pay	Cheque #
Office Salaries												
Aung, Ng	44	1,276.00		1,276.00	59.83	22.07	276.78	15.00		373.68	902.32	998
Canton, Mathew	44	1,298.00		1,298.00	60.92	22.46	283.89	20.00		387.27	910.73	999
Mueller, William	44	1,166.00		1,166.00	54.39	20.17	241.80	11.00		327.36	838.64	1024
Subtotal		10,400.00		10,400.00	452.40	179.92	2,231.21	180.00		3,043.53	7,356.47	
Wages												
Caron, Réjean	44	880.00	60.00	940.00	43.20	16.26	172.30	10.00	5.00	246.76	693.24	1025
Jordan, Mark	**48**	**880.00**	**120.00**	**1,000.00**	**46.17**	**17.30**	**191.95**	**10.00**	**5.00**	**270.42**	**729.58**	**1077**
Milroy, Lee	47	880.00	90.00	970.00	44.68	16.78	182.25	10.00	5.00	258.71	711.29	1078
Subtotal		22,000.00	2,020.00	24,020.00	1,044.88	415.55	4,491.65	300.00	150.00	6,402.08	17,617.92	
Total		32,400.00	2,020.00	34,420.00	1,497.28	595.47	6,722.86	480.00	150.00	9,445.61	24,974.39	

Note that this record is a listing of each employee's payroll data for the pay period. In some companies, the payroll register is a special journal. Postings are made directly to ledger accounts. In other companies, the payroll register is a supplementary record that gives the data for a general journal entry and later posting to the ledger accounts. At Academy Company, the second procedure is used.

In a computerized accounting system, the payroll register is automatically updated from input information on the employees' earnings records. The register also provides the supporting documentation for electronic funds transfers between the company's bank account and those of its employees. Alternatively, the register is used to generate electronically printed payroll cheques. Automatic outputs from a computerized payroll system also include monthly reports for the CRA and annual T4 slips.

Recording Payroll Expenses and Liabilities

Payroll expenses are equal to the employees' gross salaries and wages plus the employer's payroll costs. Employee payroll deductions are not an expense to the company; they are the part of an employee's gross salaries and wages that have not been paid to the employee and must instead be paid to the government or another third party. They remain a current liability to the company until they are remitted.

Employee Payroll Costs. A journal entry is made to record the employee portion of the payroll. For the week ending June 20, the entry for Academy Company, using total amounts from the company's payroll register for the period, as shown in Illustration P-12, is as follows:

A	=	L	+	OE
+6,722.86				−10,400.00
+1,497.28				−24,020.00
+595.47				
+480.00				
+150.00				
+24,974.39				

Cash flows: no effect

June 20	Salaries Expense	10,400.00	
	Wages Expense	24,020.00	
	Income Tax Payable		6,722.86
	CPP Payable		1,497.28
	EI Payable		595.47
	United Way Payable		480.00
	Union Dues Payable		150.00
	Salaries and Wages Payable		24,974.39
	To record payroll for week ending June 20.		

Specific liability accounts are credited for the required and voluntary deductions made in the pay period, as shown above. Separate expense accounts are used for gross pay because office workers are on salary and other employees are paid an hourly rate. The amount credited to Salaries and Wages Payable is the sum of the individual cheques that the employees will receive when the payroll is paid.

Employer Payroll Costs. Employer payroll costs are usually recorded when the payroll is journalized. The entire amount of gross pay is subject to four of the employer payroll costs mentioned earlier: CPP, EI, workers' compensation, and vacation pay. For the June 20 payroll, Academy Company's CPP is $1,497.28 ($1,497.28 × 1). Its EI premium is $833.66 ($595.47 × 1.4).

Assume that Academy Company is also assessed for workers' compensation at a rate of 1%. Its expense for the week would therefore be $344.20 [($10,400 + $24,020) × 1%]. For vacation pay, assume that Academy Company employees accrue vacation days at an average rate of 4% of the gross payroll (equivalent to two weeks of vacation). The accrual for vacation benefits in one pay period—one week—is therefore $1,376.80 [($10,400 + $24,020) × 4%].

Some provinces, including the Province of Ontario, require an additional employer payroll cost—an employer health tax to help fund health care. The maximum health tax in the Province of Ontario is 1.95% of payroll, but the tax rate varies by the amount of payroll and the first $400,000 of remuneration is exempt from this tax. Academy's payroll for the year has not yet reached this level so it is exempt from this health tax.

Accordingly, the entry to record the employer payroll costs or employee benefits associated with the June 20 payroll is as follows:

June 20	Employee Benefits Expense	4,051.94	
	CPP Payable		1,497.28
	EI Payable		833.66
	Workers' Compensation Payable		344.20
	Vacation Pay Payable		1,376.80
	To record employer payroll costs on June 20 payroll.		

Cash flows: no effect

These liability accounts are classified as current liabilities since they will be paid within the next year. Employee Benefits Expense is often combined with Salaries and Wages Expense on the income statement and classified as an operating expense.

Recording Payment of the Payroll

Payment of the payroll by cheque or electronic funds transfer (EFT) is made from either the employer's regular bank account or a payroll bank account. Each paycheque or EFT is usually accompanied by a statement of earnings document. This shows the employee's gross pay, payroll deductions, and net pay for the period and for the year to date.

After the payroll has been paid, the cheque numbers are entered in the payroll register. The entry to record payment of the payroll for Academy Company follows:

June 20	Salaries and Wages Payable	24,974.39	
	Cash		24,974.39
	To record payment of payroll.		

A = L + OE
−24,974.39   −24,974.39

Cash flows: −24,974.39

Many companies use a separate bank account for payroll. Only the total amount of each period's payroll is transferred, or deposited, into that account before it is distributed. This helps the company determine if there are any unclaimed amounts.

When they report and remit their payroll deductions, companies combine withholdings of income tax, CPP, and EI. Generally, the withholdings must be reported and remitted monthly on a Statement of Account for Current Source Deductions (PD7A remittance form), and no later than the 15th day of the month following the month's pay period. Depending on the size of the payroll deductions, however, the employer's payment deadline could be different. For example, large employers must remit more often than once a month through the bank, and small employers, with perfect payroll deduction remittance records, can remit quarterly. Workplace health, safety, and compensation costs are remitted quarterly to the workplace health, safety, and compensation commission. Remittances can be made by mail or through deposits at any Canadian financial institution. When payroll deductions are remitted, payroll liability accounts are debited and Cash is credited.

The entry to record the remittance of payroll deductions by Academy Company in the following month is as follows:

July 13	Income Tax Payable	6,722.86	
	CPP Payable ($1,497.28 + $1,497.28)	2,994.56	
	EI Payable ($595.47 + $833.66)	1,429.13	
	United Way Payable	480.00	
	Union Dues Payable	150.00	
	Workers' Compensation Payable	344.20	
	Cash		12,120.75
	To record payment of payroll deductions for June 20 payroll.		

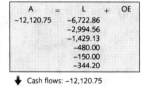

Cash flows: −12,120.75

Note that the vacation pay liability recorded on June 20 is not debited or "paid" until the employees actually take their vacation.

Other payroll information returns or forms must be filed by the employer with the government by the last day of February each year. In addition, as noted previously, employers must give employees a Statement of Remuneration Paid (T4 slip) by the same date.

Demonstration Problem

Benoit Company pays salaries on a weekly basis. The payroll for the week ending February 24, 2009, includes four employees as follows:

Employee Name	Weekly Earnings	Claim Code
Michael Blackadar	$885	4
Emily Guglielmin	$885	2
Jaegeun Kim	$1,020	1
Hua Zhang	$1,020	3

Each employee has union dues of $15. Vacation is earned at a rate of 4%. Benoit Company is assessed workers' compensation at a rate of 1% of gross payroll.

Instructions

(a) Determine the appropriate payroll deductions and net pay for each employee. Use the tables provided at the end of this supplement to determine federal and provincial income taxes. Calculate the CPP and EI deductions. Prepare a payroll register.

(b) Prepare journal entries to record:

1. The employees' portion of the February 24 payroll.
2. Benoit Company's payroll costs or employee benefits for the February 24 payroll.
3. Payment of the payroll on February 26, 2009.
4. Payment of mandatory payroll deductions on March 15, 2009.

Action Plan

- The federal tax deduction is the amount in the correct gross earnings row and in the correct claim code column on the Federal Tax Deduction Table.
- The provincial tax deduction is the amount in the correct gross earnings row and in the correct claim code column on the Provincial Tax Deduction Table.
- The CPP basic pay-period deduction is the annual basic deduction divided by the number of pay periods in a year.
- CPP deductions are equal to employee's pensionable earnings times the CPP contribution rate.
- EI premiums are equal to employee's insurable earnings times the EI premium rate.
- Employee deductions for income tax, CPP, EI, and union dues reduce the salaries payable.
- Employer contributions to CPP, EI, Workers Compensation, and vacation pay create an additional expense.
- Vacation pay is not paid until the employees take their vacation.

Solution to Demonstration Problem

(a)

Employee	Gross Pay	CPP	EI	Federal Income Tax	Provincial Income Tax	Union Dues	Total	Net Pay
Michael Blackadar	885.00	40.48[1]	15.31[3]	97.90	53.00	15.00	221.69	663.31
Emily Guglielmin	885.00	40.48	15.31	89.35	50.80	15.00	210.94	674.06
Jaegeun Kim	1,020.00	47.16[2]	17.65[4]	127.35	69.60	15.00	276.76	743.24
Hua Zhang	1,020.00	47.16	17.65	118.80	66.30	15.00	264.91	755.09
Totals	3,810.00	175.28	65.92	433.40	239.70	60.00	974.30	2,835.70

Calculations:

Note: CPP basic pay period deduction = $3,500 ÷ 52 = $67.31

1. ($885.00 − $67.31) × 4.95% = $40.48
2. ($1,020.00 − $67.31) × 4.95% = $47.16
3. $885.00 × 1.73% = $15.31
4. $1,020.00 × 1.73% = $17.65

(b)

1.	Feb. 24	Salaries Expense	3,810.00	
		CPP Payable		175.28
		EI Payable		65.92
		Income Taxes Payable ($433.40 + $239.70)		673.10
		Union Dues Payable		60.00
		Salaries Payable		2,835.70
		To record payroll for week ended February 24, 2009.		

2.	Feb. 24	Employee Benefits Expense	458.07	
		CPP Payable		175.28
		EI Payable ($65.92 × 1.40)		92.29
		Workers' Compensation Plan Payable ($3,810.00 × 1%)		38.10
		Vacation Pay Payable ($3,810.00 × 4%)		152.40
		To record employee benefit costs for February 24 payroll.		
3.	Feb. 26	Salaries Payable	2,835.70	
		Cash		2,835.70
		To record payment of the February 24 payroll.		
4.	Mar. 15	CPP Payable ($175.28 + $175.28)	350.56	
		EI Payable ($65.92 + $92.29)	158.21	
		Income Taxes Payable	673.10	
		Cash		1,181.87
		To record payment of mandatory payroll deductions.		

Glossary

Canada Pension Plan (CPP) A mandatory federal plan that gives disability, retirement, and death benefits to qualifying Canadians. (p. 2)

Employee benefits Payments made by an employer, in addition to wages and salaries, to give pension, insurance, medical, or other benefits to its employees. (p. 10)

Employee earnings record A separate record of an employee's gross pay, payroll deductions, and net pay for the calendar year that is used to prepare the employee's Statement of Remuneration Paid (T4 slip). (p. 12)

Employee payroll costs Amounts paid to employees (net pay) and amounts paid by employees (payroll deductions). (p. 1)

Employer payroll costs Amounts paid by the employer on behalf of the employee. Also called employee benefits. (p. 1)

Employment Insurance (EI) A federal mandatory insurance program designed to give income protection for a limited period of time to employees who are temporarily laid off, who are on parental leave, or who lose their jobs. (p. 3)

Gross pay Total compensation earned by an employee. Also known as gross earnings. (p. 1)

Insurable earnings Gross earnings. (p. 4)

Net pay Gross pay less payroll deductions. (p. 10)

Payroll deductions Deductions from gross pay to determine the amount of a paycheque. (p. 2)

Payroll deduction tables Tables prepared by the CRA showing the income taxes, CPP, and EI amounts to be withheld from employees' wages at various levels of earnings. (p. 5)

Payroll register A record that accumulates the gross pay, deductions, and net pay per employee for each pay period and becomes the documentation for preparing a paycheque for each employee. (p. 13)

Pensionable earnings Gross earnings less the basic yearly exemption. (p. 3)

Personal tax credits Amounts that may be claimed on an individual's income tax return to reduce income taxes; also used to determine the amount of income taxes to be withheld. (p. 4)

Standard work week The number of hours that an hourly worker needs to have worked before overtime becomes payable. (p. 1)

TD1 A form completed by an employee to calculate the total amount of personal tax credits based on their best estimate of their circumstances. Also known as the Personal Tax Credits Return. (p. 4)

Self-Study Questions

Answers are at the end of the chapter.

1. Rebecca works for The Blue Company at a salary of $550 per week. Canada Pension Plan contributions are $23.89 for the employee and the same for the employer. Income taxes are $87.80. Employment insurance premiums are $9.52 for the employee and $13.33 for the employer. How much is Rebecca's weekly net pay (i.e., her take-home pay)?
   (a) $390.49   (c) $414.38
   (b) $428.79   (d) $424.67

2. During a recent week, Emilie Marquette worked 35 hours at an hourly wage of $20 per hour. Assume the basic yearly exemption is $3,500, and the CPP contribution rate is 4.95%. Assume the EI premium rate is 1.73%. The employee's and employer's share of CPP and EI are:
   (a) employee CPP, $31.32; EI, $12.11; employer CPP, $31.32; EI, $12.11.
   (b) employee CPP, $31.32; EI, $12.11; employer CPP, $31.32; EI, $16.95.
   (c) employee CPP, $43.85; EI, $12.11; employer CPP, $43.85; EI, $16.95.
   (d) employee CPP, $31.32; EI, $12.11; employer CPP, $31.86; EI, $12.11.

Questions

1. What is the difference between salaries and wages?

2. Explain the different types of employee and employer payroll deductions, and give examples of each.

3. How is the amount deducted from an employee's wages for income tax determined?

4. What is the purpose of the TD1 form?

5. Explain how CPP is calculated.

6. Explain how EI is calculated.

7. What is the difference between gross pay and net pay? Which amount (gross or net) should a company record as salaries and wages expense?

8. What are three payroll deduction tools available from CRA? How often are these tools updated?

9. Explain the difference between employee payroll costs and employer payroll costs.

10. What are an employee earnings record and a payroll register?

11. To whom, and how often, are payroll deductions remitted?

12. What is the Statement of Remuneration Paid (T4)? What information is include on a T4 and how often is a T4 prepared?

13. Identify employee benefits that must be paid for by employers. Identify employee benefits that can be paid for by employers. How are both accounted for?

Brief Exercises

BEP–1   Becky Sherrick's regular hourly wage rate is $18.50 and she receives an hourly rate of $27.75 for work over 40 hours per week. In the week ended January 15, 2009, Becky worked 49.5 hours. Calculate Becky's gross pay.

BEP–2   Refer to information for Becky Sherrick in BEP–1. Calculate Becky's CPP and EI deductions.

BEP–3   Refer to information for Becky Sherrick in BEP–1. Using Illustrations P–6 and P–7, locate the correct pay range and related CPP and EI deductions. Compare with your answer in BEP–2.

BEP–4   Refer to information for Becky Sherrick in BEP–1. Assume that Becky is a resident of Ontario and Becky's TD1 indicates Claim Code 2. Using Illustrations P–4 and P–5, locate the correct pay range and related federal and provincial income tax deductions.

BEP–5   Refer to information for Becky Sherrick in BEP–1 to BEP–4. (a) Calculate Becky's net pay. (b) Prepare the journal entry to record Becky's pay for the period, assuming she was paid on January 15.

BEP–6   The following is a list of payroll costs. For each payroll cost identified, determine if the cost is mandatory or voluntary. As well, determine if the cost will be a deduction to the employee and/or an expense to the employer.

	Mandatory/Voluntary	Deduction to the employee	Expense to the employer
Canada Pension Plan			
Charitable donations			
Union dues			
Medical insurance			
Employment insurance			
Federal income tax			
Provincial income tax			
Private pension plan			
Workers' compensation			

BEP–7   Katy Anderson is a new employee of SKLD Consulting Ltd. located in Ontario, and has negotiated an annual salary of $52,000. Katy is paid biweekly. According to the Payroll Deductions Online Calculator, federal tax deductions are $246.75; provincial tax deductions are $134.86; CPP deductions are $92.34; and EI deductions are $34.60. Calculate (a) Katy's gross and net pay, and (b) SKLD's contribution for CPP and EI.

BEP–8   Zerbe Consulting Company's gross salaries for the week ending August 22 were $25,000. Deductions included $1,234 for CPP, $433 for EI, and $8,233 for income taxes. The company's payroll costs were $1,234 for CPP and $606 for EI. Prepare journal entries to record (a) the employee payroll costs, assuming salaries were paid August 22, (b) the employer payroll costs, and (c) the remittance on September 15.

BEP–9   In January, the gross pay in Bri Company totalled $60,000, from which $2,118 was deducted for Canada Pension, $732 for employment insurance, and $22,309 for income tax. (a) Prepare the journal entries to record January payroll, including employee benefit costs. (b) Prepare journal entries for the payment of payroll on January 31 and the payment of payroll deductions on February 15.

BEP–10   Martina Hernandez earned $60,000 in 2009 and was paid on a monthly basis. She worked for HillSide Tours for all of 2009. What were her CPP and EI deductions in (a) January 2009 and (b) December 2009?

BEP–11   Fill in the missing amounts of Western Classic Vehicle Restoration's payroll register prepared for the month ended October 31.

Administrative salaries	$55,000	CPP deductions	$ 3,570
EI deductions	2,350	Technicians' wages	(a)
Income tax	(b)	Total deductions	28,665
Total gross pay	75,000	Net pay	(c)

Exercises

EP–1   On June 1, 2009, Janet Dufour was hired as the manager of Aspinall Appraisals Ltd. at an annual salary of $58,000. Calculate the semi-monthly CPP contribution and EI premium that must be deducted from Janet's gross pay.

EP–2   Refer to information for Janet Dufour in EP–1. Calculate the bi-weekly CPP contribution and EI premium that must be deducted from Janet's gross pay.

EP–3   Sunan's Deliveries Ltd. has two salaried employees, Shelley Irvine, the manager, and Lee Anderson, the administrator. Both employees are celebrating their 10-year anniversaries with the company. Employees are paid monthly. Shelley is paid $4,200 per month and Lee is paid $2,300 per month. Calculate the monthly CPP contributions and EI contributions that must be deducted from each of Sunan's employees for the months of November and December, 2009.

EP–4   Chandra Durji is the owner of a flower shop, Flowers Unlimited. Her assistant manager, Sonia Palese, earns an annual salary of $51,900. The company also employs a full-time assistant, Billy Brown, who is paid $18 per hour. Both employees are paid biweekly.

In the pay period ended May 31, 2009, Billy has worked 95 hours and is paid time and one half for hours worked in excess of 80. Both employees are residents of Ontario. Billy has a claim code of 4 for tax deductions. Sonia has a claim code of 1 for tax deductions.

Instructions

Using payroll tables provided on pages 27–30 determine gross and net pay for each employee.
   (a) Prepare the journal entry for salaries and wages on May 31, 2009, assuming that the salaries and wages were also paid on this date.
   (b) Prepare the journal entry to record Flowers Unlimited's related payroll costs on May 31, 2009, assuming they were not paid on this date.

EP–5   Kate Gough's regular hourly wage rate is $13 and she receives a wage of 1.5 times the regular hourly rate for work over 40 hours per week. For the week ending May 26, 2009, Kate worked 45 hours. Kate lives in Alberta and has a claim code of 1 for tax deductions. After this information is inputted into the Payroll Deductions Online Calculator (PDOC), the following information is generated:

■◆■ Canada Revenue Agency Agence du revenu du Canada	**Canadä**

Payroll Deductions Online Calculator

Results - Effective April 1, 2009

Employee's name	Kate Gough
Employer's name	
Pay period	Weekly (52 pay periods a year)
Pay period ending date	2009-05-26
Province of employment	Alberta
Federal amount from TD1	Claim Code 1 (Minimum - 10,375.00)
Provincial amount from TD1	Claim Code 1 (Minimum - 16,775.00)
Salary or wages for the pay period	617.50
Total EI insurable earnings for the pay period	617.50
Taxable income	617.50
Cash income for the pay period	617.50
Federal tax deductions	54.00
Provincial tax deductions	25.70
Requested additional tax deduction	0.00
Total tax on income	79.70
CPP deductions	27.23
EI deductions	10.68
Amounts deducted at source	0.00
Total deductions on income	117.61
Net amount	499.89

Instructions

(a) Show how Kate's gross pay was calculated.

(b) Kate also has a voluntary deduction of $5 for the United Way each week. Calculate Kate's net pay for the pay period ending May 26, 2009.

(c) Prepare the journal entry for Kate's wages on May 26, 2009, assuming that the wages were also paid on this date.

(d) Prepare the journal entry to record the employer's related payroll costs on May 26, assuming they were not paid on this date.

EP–6   Hidden Dragon Restaurant's gross payroll for August is $38,500. The company deducted $1,715 for CPP, $666 for EI, and $6,010 for income taxes from the employees' cheques. Employees are paid monthly at the end of each month. Hidden Dragon's related payroll costs for August are $1,715 for CPP and $932 for EI.

Instructions

(a) Prepare the journal entry for Hidden Dragon on August 31 to record the payment of the August payroll to employees.

(b) Prepare a journal entry on August 31 to accrue Hidden Dragon's employer payroll costs.

(c) On September 15, Hidden Dragon pays the government the correct amounts for August's payroll. Prepare a journal entry to record this remittance.

EP–7   In April, the gross pay of Space Ride Investments Ltd. totalled $64,000, from which $2,995 was deducted for Canada Pension, $1,107 for employment insurance, and $24,935 for income tax. Each of the 20 employees pays union dues of $15. Vacation pay is earned at a rate of 4%. Space Ride is assessed workers' compensation at a rate of 1.5% of gross payroll.

Instructions

(a) Prepare journal entries to record the employees' portion of the April 30 payroll, assuming that the salaries and wages were also paid on this date.

(b) Prepare journal entries to record Space Ride's payroll costs for the April 30 payroll, assuming they were not paid on this date. Round all amounts to the nearest dollar.

(c) Upon analysis of journal entries prepared in (a) and (b) above, what are Space Ride's total payroll expenses incurred? Will all of these expenses result in a decrease in cash?

EP–8   Ahmad Company has the following data for the weekly payroll ending January 27, 2009:

	Hours Worked						Hourly	Income Tax	Health
Employee	M	Tu	W	Th	F	S	Rate	Withheld	Insurance
A. Kassam	8	8	9	8	10	3	$16.00	$ 81.00	$20.00
H. Faas	8	8	8	8	8	2	18.00	87.00	25.00
G. Labute	9	10	8	8	9	0	20.00	107.00	25.00

Employees are paid 1.5 times the regular hourly rate for all hours worked over 40 hours per week. Ahmad Company must make payments to the workers' compensation plan equal to 2% of the gross payroll. In addition, Ahmad matches the employee's health insurance contributions.

Instructions

(a) Calculate each employee's regular and overtime gross pay.

(b) Calculate CPP and EI deductions for each employee using 2009 rates.

(c) Prepare the payroll register for the weekly payroll.

(d) Prepare journal entries to record payroll and Ahmad Company's benefits. Assume that wages were paid on January 27 and Ahmad's benefits were not paid on this date.

EP–9   Selected data from the November 28 payroll register for Yue Company follow, with some amounts missing:

Gross pay:		Deductions:	
Regular	$ (2)	Canada Pension Plan	$ (3)
Overtime	1,050	Employment insurance	219
Total	(1)	Income tax	3,389
		Union dues	139
		United Way	225
		Total deductions	(4)
		Net pay	(5)
		Accounts Debited:	
		Warehouse wages expense	5,070
		Store wages expense	(6)

Pensionable earnings are $12,000. CPP premiums are 4.95% of pensionable earnings. EI premiums are 1.73% of gross pay.

Instructions

(a) Fill in the missing amounts. Round all answers to the nearest dollar.
(b) Calculate the company's contributions to the Canada Pension Plan and employment insurance. Round all amounts to the nearest dollar.
(c) Record all payroll amounts. Assume employees were paid on Nov. 28.
(d) Record the payment of amounts withheld, assuming they were paid on Dec. 10.

Problems: Set A

PP–1A   Scoot Scooter has four employees who are paid on an hourly basis, plus time and one half for hours in excess of 40 per week. Payroll data for the week ended May 18, 2009, follow:

Employee	Total Hours	Hourly Rate	Income Tax	United Way
P. Kilchyk	40	$12.50	$55.05	$0.00
B. Quon	42	14.00	67.10	5.00
C. Pospisil	45	16.50	84.15	7.50
B. Verwey	44	13.50	75.10	5.00

Instructions

(a) Calculate gross pay, CPP, and EI deductions for each employee.
(b) Prepare a payroll register for the weekly payroll.
(c) Record the payroll on May 18, and the accrual of employee benefits expense. Assume employees are paid on May 18.
(d) Record the payment of the employee benefits on June 15.

PP–2A   Minh Bo Ltd. has two employees who are paid on an hourly basis plus time and one half for hours worked in excess of 80 hours on a biweekly basis. Payroll data for the two-week period ended March 31, 2009, follow:

Employee	Total Hours	Hourly Rate	TD 1 Claim	Medical Insurance Deduction
A. Thal	85	$21.50	2	$25
D. Parkins	81	$23.00	3	$15

Vacation pay is earned at a rate of 4%. Minh Bo Ltd. is assessed workers' compensation at a rate of 2% of gross payroll. Minh Bo matches the amount of medical insurance each employee pays. All employees are residents of Ontario.

Instructions

(a) Calculate gross pay and prepare a payroll register using the appropriate payroll deduction tables on pages 27–30.
(b) From the payroll register prepare the journal entry to record the employee portion of the March 31 payroll. Assume employees are paid on April 2.
(c) From the payroll register prepare the journal entry to record the employer portion of the March 31 payroll.
(d) Prepare the journal entry to record the payment of payroll on April 2.
(e) Prepare the journal entry to record the payment of payroll deductions April 15.

PP–3A Maxim Resources has two salaried employees. John Craig, the Human Resources Manager, earns $76,400 per year. Maggie Smith, the Investor Relations Manager, earns $88,200 per year. Employees are paid semi-monthly.

Instructions

(a) For each employee calculate the CPP and EI deductions for a semi-monthly pay period using 2009 rates.
(b) For each employee determine the pay period where the maximum CPP contribution has been reached and the amount to be deducted that period.
(c) For each employee determine the pay period where the maximum EI contribution has been reached.
(d) Assume that on August 15 John is given a raise and is now earning $80,000 per year. Determine when his maximum CPP contribution and EI contribution will be reached.

PP–4A The following payroll liability accounts are included in the ledger of Amora Company on January 1, 2010:

Canada Pension Plan payable	$8,788	Union dues payable	$1,400
Canada Savings Bonds payable	2,420	United Way donations payable	750
Employment insurance payable	4,768	Vacation pay payable	9,704
Income tax payable	35,510	Workers' compensation payable	4,676

In January, the following transactions occurred:

Jan. 10 Sent a cheque to the union treasurer for union dues.
    12 Issued a cheque to the Receiver General for the amounts due for CPP, EI, and income tax.
    17 Issued a cheque to United Way.
    20 Paid the workers' compensation plan.
    31 Prepared the monthly payroll register, which showed office salaries $41,800; store wages $48,400; income tax withheld $20,400; CPP withheld $4,127; EI withheld $1,668; union dues withheld $1,450; United Way contributions $750; and Canada Savings Bonds deductions $1,210.
    31 Prepared payroll cheques for the net pay and distributed them to employees.

At January 31, the company also made the following adjusting entries for employee benefits:

1. The employer's share of CPP and EI
2. Workers' compensation plan at 6% of gross pay
3. Vacation pay at 4% of gross pay

Instructions

(a) Enter the beginning balances in general ledger accounts.
(b) Record and post the January transactions and adjustments.

PP–5A   Selected data follow from a payroll register for the week ended June 30 for Slovac Company, with some amounts missing:

Store wages expense	$ (a)	United Way	$ 270
Warehouse wages expense	7,800	Income tax	(c)
CPP deductions	1,165	Net pay	10,410
EI deductions	(b)	Overtime earnings	490
Group insurance plan	390	Regular earnings	23,150
Union dues	260	Total gross pay	(d)

Instructions

(a) Fill in the missing amounts. Round all answers to the nearest dollar.
(b) Record the payroll, including the employer's portion of CPP and EI, for the week ended June 30.
(c) Record the payment of the payroll to the employees on June 30, and the remittance of the amounts due to the Receiver General on July 15.

Problems: Set B

PP–1B   Sure Value Hardware has four employees who are paid on an hourly basis, plus time and one half for hours worked in excess of 40 hours a week. Payroll data for the week ended March 16, 2009, follow:

Employee	Total Hours	Hourly Rate	Income Tax	United Way
I. Dahl	41	$15.00	$109.79	5.00
F. Gualtieri	42	15.00	99.35	5.00
G. Ho	48	14.50	168.00	18.00
A. Israeli	46	14.50	122.75	5.00

The first three employees are sales clerks (store wages expense) and the other employee does administrative duties (office wages expense).

Instructions

(a) Calculate gross pay, CPP, and EI deductions for each employee.
(b) Prepare a payroll register for the weekly payroll.
(c) Record the payroll on March 16, and the accrual of employee benefits expense.
(d) Record the payment of the payroll on March 16.
(e) Record the payment of employee benefits on April 15.

PP–2B   Walk a Doggie has three employees who are paid on an hourly basis plus time and one half for hours worked in excess of 80 hours biweekly. Payroll data for the two-week period ended May 31, 2009, follow:

Employee	Total Hours	Rate per Hour	TD 1 Claim	Medical Insurance Deduction	Donation to the SPCA
A. Turner	90	$20.00	3	$25	$8
D. Grath	84	$21.50	2	$15	$5
J. Paul	81	$23.00	1	$15	$5

Vacation pay is earned at a rate of 4%. Walk a Doggie is assessed workers' compensation at a rate of 3% of gross payroll. Walk a Doggie matches the amount of medical insurance each employee pays.

Instructions

(a) Calculate gross pay and prepare a payroll register using the appropriate payroll deduction tables on pages 27–30.

(b) From the payroll register prepare the journal entry to record the employee portion of the May 31 payroll. Assume employees are paid on June 1.

(c) From the payroll register prepare the journal entry to record the employer portion of the May 31 payroll.

(d) Prepare the journal entry to record the payment of payroll on June 1.

(e) Prepare the journal entry to record the payment of payroll deductions to the Receiver General on June 15 and to the medical insurance provider on June 20.

PP–3B Glames Drilling has two salaried employees. Perry Ackerman, the Drilling Supervisor, earns $55,000 per year. June Vosburgh, the IT Manager, earns $79,000 per year. Employees are paid monthly.

Instructions

(a) For each employee calculate the CPP and EI deductions for a monthly pay period using 2009 rates.

(b) For each employee determine the pay period where the maximum CPP contribution has been reached and the amount to be deducted that period.

(c) For each employee determine the pay period where the maximum EI contribution has been reached and the amount to be deducted that period.

(d) Assume that on September 1, 2009, June is given a raise and is now earning $82,000 per year. Recalculate her monthly CPP deduction and EI deductions and re-determine when her maximum CPP contribution and EI contribution will be reached.

PP–4B The following payroll liability accounts are included in the ledger of Drumheller Company on January 1, 2010:

Canada Pension Plan payable	$5,454	Income tax payable	$28,600
Canada Savings Bonds payable	2,500	Union dues payable	1,250
Disability insurance payable	3,050	Vacation pay payable	16,450
Employment insurance payable	2,923	Workers' compensation payable	2,263

In January, the following transactions occurred:

Jan. 8 Sent a cheque to the insurance company for the disability insurance.

10 Sent a cheque for $1,250 to the union treasurer for union dues.

12 Issued a cheque to the Receiver General for the amounts due for CPP, EI, and income tax.

15 Purchased Canada Savings Bonds for employees by writing a cheque for $2,500.

20 Paid the amount due to the workers' compensation plan.

31 Completed the monthly payroll register, which shows office salaries $46,400; store wages $37,400; income tax withheld $22,760; CPP withheld $3,014; EI withheld $1,193; union dues withheld $950; Canada Savings Bond deductions $1,200; and long-term disability insurance premiums $3,100.

31 Prepared payroll cheques for the net pay and distributed the cheques to the employees.

At January 31, the company also made the following adjusting entries for employee benefits:

1. The employer's share of CPP and EI
2. Workers' compensation plan at 3% of gross pay
3. Vacation pay at 4% of gross pay

Instructions

(a) Enter the beginning balances in general ledger accounts.
(b) Journalize and post the January transactions and adjustments.
(c) Calculate ending balances for each account at January 31, 2010.

PP–5B   Selected data follow from a payroll register for the week ended December 31 for Western Electric Company, with some amounts missing:

Administrative salaries	$ (a)	Long-term disability insurance	$ 14,500
CPP deductions	28,710	Net pay	357,235
Dental insurance premiums	6,400	Total deductions	(b)
EI deductions	12,155	Total gross pay	(c)
Electricians' wages	370,000	United Way contributions	6,000
Income tax	93,000		

In addition to CPP and EI, Western Electric Company's employee benefits include matching the employees' contributions to the dental and long-term disability insurance plans and paying workers' compensation of $26,000.

Instructions

(a) Fill in the missing amounts. Round all answers to the nearest dollar.
(b) Record the payroll, including employee benefits, for the week ended December 31.
(c) Record the payment of the payroll to the employees on December 31, and the remittance of the amounts due to third parties on January 15.

ANSWERS TO CHAPTER QUESTIONS

Answer to Accounting in Action Insight Question

All About You, p. 11

Q: If you are providing services to a company, what are the financial advantages and disadvantages of being a self-employed consultant versus an employee of the company?

A: CAs a self-employed individual, your monthly cash received from the company would be higher as no CPP, EI, and income tax will be deducted. On the other hand, you will have to make quarterly instalment payments of CPP, EI (if you choose to pay it) and income taxes. If you are self-employed, you may be able to deduct certain expenses to reduce your income tax. However, some individuals may not manage their cash properly and may be unable to make the remittances when required. In addition, you will have to pay twice as much for CPP and you will not qualify for EI benefits. If you are self-employed, you would not qualify for other benefits offered to employees by the company either.

Answers to Self-Study Questions

1. b   2. b

Employment Insurance Premiums

Cotisations à l'assurance-emploi

Insurable Earnings Rémunération assurable From - De	To - À	EI premium Cotisation d'AE	Insurable Earnings Rémunération assurable From - De	To - À	EI premium Cotisation d'AE	Insurable Earnings Rémunération assurable From - De	To - À	EI premium Cotisation d'AE	Insurable Earnings Rémunération assurable From - De	To - À	EI premium Cotisation d'AE
1831.51	1832.08	31.69	1873.13	1873.69	32.41	1914.74	1915.31	33.13	1956.36	1956.93	33.85
1832.09	1832.65	31.70	1873.70	1874.27	32.42	1915.32	1915.89	33.14	1956.94	1957.51	33.86
1832.66	1833.23	31.71	1874.28	1874.85	32.43	1915.90	1916.47	33.15	1957.52	1958.09	33.87
1833.24	1833.81	31.72	1874.86	1875.43	32.44	1916.48	1917.05	33.16	1958.10	1958.67	33.88
1833.82	1834.39	31.73	1875.44	1876.01	32.45	1917.06	1917.63	33.17	1958.68	1959.24	33.89
1834.40	1834.97	31.74	1876.02	1876.58	32.46	1917.64	1918.20	33.18	1959.25	1959.82	33.90
1834.98	1835.54	31.75	1876.59	1877.16	32.47	1918.21	1918.78	33.19	1959.83	1960.40	33.91
1835.55	1836.12	31.76	1877.17	1877.74	32.48	1918.79	1919.36	33.20	1960.41	1960.98	33.92
1836.13	1836.70	31.77	1877.75	1878.32	32.49	1919.37	1919.94	33.21	1960.99	1961.56	33.93
1836.71	1837.28	31.78	1878.33	1878.90	32.50	1919.95	1920.52	33.22	1961.57	1962.13	33.94
1837.29	1837.86	31.79	1878.91	1879.47	32.51	1920.53	1921.09	33.23	1962.14	1962.71	33.95
1837.87	1838.43	31.80	1879.48	1880.05	32.52	1921.10	1921.67	33.24	1962.72	1963.29	33.96
1838.44	1839.01	31.81	1880.06	1880.63	32.53	1921.68	1922.25	33.25	1963.30	1963.87	33.97
1839.02	1839.59	31.82	1880.64	1881.21	32.54	1922.26	1922.83	33.26	1963.88	1964.45	33.98
1839.60	1840.17	31.83	1881.22	1881.79	32.55	1922.84	1923.41	33.27	1964.46	1965.02	33.99
1840.18	1840.75	31.84	1881.80	1882.36	32.56	1923.42	1923.98	33.28	1965.03	1965.60	34.00
1840.76	1841.32	31.85	1882.37	1882.94	32.57	1923.99	1924.56	33.29	1965.61	1966.18	34.01
1841.33	1841.90	31.86	1882.95	1883.52	32.58	1924.57	1925.14	33.30	1966.19	1966.76	34.02
1841.91	1842.48	31.87	1883.53	1884.10	32.59	1925.15	1925.72	33.31	1966.77	1967.34	34.03
1842.49	1843.06	31.88	1884.11	1884.68	32.60	1925.73	1926.30	33.32	1967.35	1967.91	34.04
1843.07	1843.64	31.89	1884.69	1885.26	32.61	1926.31	1926.87	33.33	1967.92	1968.49	34.05
1843.65	1844.21	31.90	1885.27	1885.83	32.62	1926.88	1927.45	33.34	1968.50	1969.07	34.06
1844.22	1844.79	31.91	1885.84	1886.41	32.63	1927.46	1928.03	33.35	1969.08	1969.65	34.07
1844.80	1845.37	31.92	1886.42	1886.99	32.64	1928.04	1928.61	33.36	1969.66	1970.23	34.08
1845.38	1845.95	31.93	1887.00	1887.57	32.65	1928.62	1929.19	33.37	1970.24	1970.80	34.09
1845.96	1846.53	31.94	1887.58	1888.15	32.66	1929.20	1929.76	33.38	1970.81	1971.38	34.10
1846.54	1847.10	31.95	1888.16	1888.72	32.67	1929.77	1930.34	33.39	1971.39	1971.96	34.11
1847.11	1847.68	31.96	1888.73	1889.30	32.68	1930.35	1930.92	33.40	1971.97	1972.54	34.12
1847.69	1848.26	31.97	1889.31	1889.88	32.69	1930.93	1931.50	33.41	1972.55	1973.12	34.13
1848.27	1848.84	31.98	1889.89	1890.46	32.70	1931.51	1932.08	33.42	1973.13	1973.69	34.14
1848.85	1849.42	31.99	1890.47	1891.04	32.71	1932.09	1932.65	33.43	1973.70	1974.27	34.15
1849.43	1849.99	32.00	1891.05	1891.61	32.72	1932.66	1933.23	33.44	1974.28	1974.85	34.16
1850.00	1850.57	32.01	1891.62	1892.19	32.73	1933.24	1933.81	33.45	1974.86	1975.43	34.17
1850.58	1851.15	32.02	1892.20	1892.77	32.74	1933.82	1934.39	33.46	1975.44	1976.01	34.18
1851.16	1851.73	32.03	1892.78	1893.35	32.75	1934.40	1934.97	33.47	1976.02	1976.58	34.19
1851.74	1852.31	32.04	1893.36	1893.93	32.76	1934.98	1935.54	33.48	1976.59	1977.16	34.20
1852.32	1852.89	32.05	1893.94	1894.50	32.77	1935.55	1936.12	33.49	1977.17	1977.74	34.21
1852.90	1853.46	32.06	1894.51	1895.08	32.78	1936.13	1936.70	33.50	1977.75	1978.32	34.22
1853.47	1854.04	32.07	1895.09	1895.66	32.79	1936.71	1937.28	33.51	1978.33	1978.90	34.23
1854.05	1854.62	32.08	1895.67	1896.24	32.80	1937.29	1937.86	33.52	1978.91	1979.47	34.24
1854.63	1855.20	32.09	1896.25	1896.82	32.81	1937.87	1938.43	33.53	1979.48	1980.05	34.25
1855.21	1855.78	32.10	1896.83	1897.39	32.82	1938.44	1939.01	33.54	1980.06	1980.63	34.26
1855.79	1856.35	32.11	1897.40	1897.97	32.83	1939.02	1939.59	33.55	1980.64	1981.21	34.27
1856.36	1856.93	32.12	1897.98	1898.55	32.84	1939.60	1940.17	33.56	1981.22	1981.79	34.28
1856.94	1857.51	32.13	1898.56	1899.13	32.85	1940.18	1940.75	33.57	1981.80	1982.36	34.29
1857.52	1858.09	32.14	1899.14	1899.71	32.86	1940.76	1941.32	33.58	1982.37	1982.94	34.30
1858.10	1858.67	32.15	1899.72	1900.28	32.87	1941.33	1941.90	33.59	1982.95	1983.52	34.31
1858.68	1859.24	32.16	1900.29	1900.86	32.88	1941.91	1942.48	33.60	1983.53	1984.10	34.32
1859.25	1859.82	32.17	1900.87	1901.44	32.89	1942.49	1943.06	33.61	1984.11	1984.68	34.33
1859.83	1860.40	32.18	1901.45	1902.02	32.90	1943.07	1943.64	33.62	1984.69	1985.26	34.34
1860.41	1860.98	32.19	1902.03	1902.60	32.91	1943.65	1944.21	33.63	1985.27	1985.83	34.35
1860.99	1861.56	32.20	1902.61	1903.17	32.92	1944.22	1944.79	33.64	1985.84	1986.41	34.36
1861.57	1862.13	32.21	1903.18	1903.75	32.93	1944.80	1945.37	33.65	1986.42	1986.99	34.37
1862.14	1862.71	32.22	1903.76	1904.33	32.94	1945.38	1945.95	33.66	1987.00	1987.57	34.38
1862.72	1863.29	32.23	1904.34	1904.91	32.95	1945.96	1946.53	33.67	1987.58	1988.15	34.39
1863.30	1863.87	32.24	1904.92	1905.49	32.96	1946.54	1947.10	33.68	1988.16	1988.72	34.40
1863.88	1864.45	32.25	1905.50	1906.06	32.97	1947.11	1947.68	33.69	1988.73	1989.30	34.41
1864.46	1865.02	32.26	1906.07	1906.64	32.98	1947.69	1948.26	33.70	1989.31	1989.88	34.42
1865.03	1865.60	32.27	1906.65	1907.22	32.99	1948.27	1948.84	33.71	1989.89	1990.46	34.43
1865.61	1866.18	32.28	1907.23	1907.80	33.00	1948.85	1949.42	33.72	1990.47	1991.04	34.44
1866.19	1866.76	32.29	1907.81	1908.38	33.01	1949.43	1949.99	33.73	1991.05	1991.61	34.45
1866.77	1867.34	32.30	1908.39	1908.95	33.02	1950.00	1950.57	33.74	1991.62	1992.19	34.46
1867.35	1867.91	32.31	1908.96	1909.53	33.03	1950.58	1951.15	33.75	1992.20	1992.77	34.47
1867.92	1868.49	32.32	1909.54	1910.11	33.04	1951.16	1951.73	33.76	1992.78	1993.35	34.48
1868.50	1869.07	32.33	1910.12	1910.69	33.05	1951.74	1952.31	33.77	1993.36	1993.93	34.49
1869.08	1869.65	32.34	1910.70	1911.27	33.06	1952.32	1952.89	33.78	1993.94	1994.50	34.50
1869.66	1870.23	32.35	1911.28	1911.84	33.07	1952.90	1953.46	33.79	1994.51	1995.08	34.51
1870.24	1870.80	32.36	1911.85	1912.42	33.08	1953.47	1954.04	33.80	1995.09	1995.66	34.52
1870.81	1871.38	32.37	1912.43	1913.00	33.09	1954.05	1954.62	33.81	1995.67	1996.24	34.53
1871.39	1871.96	32.38	1913.01	1913.58	33.10	1954.63	1955.20	33.82	1996.25	1996.82	34.54
1871.97	1872.54	32.39	1913.59	1914.16	33.11	1955.21	1955.78	33.83	1996.83	1997.39	34.55
1872.55	1873.12	32.40	1914.17	1914.73	33.12	1955.79	1956.35	33.84	1997.40	1997.97	34.56

Yearly maximum insurable earnings are $42,300
Yearly maximum employee premiums are $731.79
The premium rate for 2009 is 1.73 %

Le maximum annuel de la rémunération assurable est de 42 300 $
La cotisation maximale annuelle de l'employé est de 731,79 $
Le taux de cotisation pour 2009 est de 1,73 %

Federal tax deductions
Effective April 1, 2009
Biweekly (26 pay periods a year)
**Also look up the tax deductions
in the provincial table**

Retenues d'impôt fédéral
En vigueur le 1er avril 2009
Aux deux semaines (26 périodes de paie par année)
**Cherchez aussi les retenues d'impôt
dans la table provinciale**

Pay / Rémunération		Federal claim codes/Codes de demande fédéraux										
		0	1	2	3	4	5	6	7	8	9	10
From De	Less than Moins de	Deduct from each pay / Retenez sur chaque paie										
1120	1136	152.85	93.00	87.35	75.95	64.60	53.20	41.80	30.45	19.05	7.70	
1136	1152	155.10	95.25	89.55	78.20	66.80	55.45	44.05	32.70	21.30	9.95	
1152	1168	157.35	97.50	91.80	80.45	69.05	57.70	46.30	34.90	23.55	12.15	.80
1168	1184	159.60	99.75	94.05	82.65	71.30	59.90	48.55	37.15	25.80	14.40	3.05
1184	1200	161.85	102.00	96.30	84.90	73.55	62.15	50.80	39.40	28.05	16.65	5.25
1200	1216	164.05	104.20	98.55	87.15	75.75	64.40	53.00	41.65	30.25	18.90	7.50
1216	1232	166.30	106.45	100.75	89.40	78.00	66.65	55.25	43.90	32.50	21.15	9.75
1232	1248	168.55	108.70	103.00	91.65	80.25	68.90	57.50	46.10	34.75	23.35	12.00
1248	1264	170.80	110.95	105.25	93.85	82.50	71.10	59.75	48.35	37.00	25.60	14.25
1264	1280	173.05	113.20	107.50	96.10	84.75	73.35	62.00	50.60	39.25	27.85	16.45
1280	1296	175.25	115.40	109.75	98.35	86.95	75.60	64.20	52.85	41.45	30.10	18.70
1296	1312	177.50	117.65	111.95	100.60	89.20	77.85	66.45	55.10	43.70	32.35	20.95
1312	1328	179.75	119.90	114.20	102.85	91.45	80.10	68.70	57.30	45.95	34.55	23.20
1328	1344	182.00	122.15	116.45	105.05	93.70	82.30	70.95	59.55	48.20	36.80	25.45
1344	1360	184.25	124.35	118.70	107.30	95.95	84.55	73.20	61.80	50.40	39.05	27.65
1360	1376	186.45	126.60	120.90	109.55	98.15	86.80	75.40	64.05	52.65	41.30	29.90
1376	1392	188.70	128.85	123.15	111.80	100.40	89.05	77.65	66.30	54.90	43.55	32.15
1392	1408	190.95	131.10	125.40	114.05	102.65	91.25	79.90	68.50	57.15	45.75	34.40
1408	1424	193.20	133.35	127.65	116.25	104.90	93.50	82.15	70.75	59.40	48.00	36.65
1424	1440	195.45	135.55	129.90	118.50	107.15	95.75	84.40	73.00	61.60	50.25	38.85
1440	1456	197.65	137.80	132.10	120.75	109.35	98.00	86.60	75.25	63.85	52.50	41.10
1456	1472	199.90	140.05	134.35	123.00	111.60	100.25	88.85	77.50	66.10	54.70	43.35
1472	1488	202.15	142.30	136.60	125.25	113.85	102.45	91.10	79.70	68.35	56.95	45.60
1488	1504	204.40	144.55	138.85	127.45	116.10	104.70	93.35	81.95	70.60	59.20	47.85
1504	1520	206.65	146.75	141.10	129.70	118.35	106.95	95.55	84.20	72.80	61.45	50.05
1520	1536	208.85	149.00	143.30	131.95	120.55	109.20	97.80	86.45	75.05	63.70	52.30
1536	1552	211.10	151.25	145.55	134.20	122.80	111.45	100.05	88.70	77.30	65.90	54.55
1552	1568	213.35	153.50	147.80	136.40	125.05	113.65	102.30	90.90	79.55	68.15	56.80
1568	1584	215.60	155.75	150.05	138.65	127.30	115.90	104.55	93.15	81.80	70.40	59.05
1584	1600	218.35	158.50	152.80	141.40	130.05	118.65	107.30	95.90	84.55	73.15	61.80
1600	1616	221.70	161.85	156.15	144.80	133.40	122.05	110.65	99.25	87.90	76.50	65.15
1616	1632	225.05	165.20	159.50	148.15	136.75	125.40	114.00	102.65	91.25	79.90	68.50
1632	1648	228.45	168.60	162.90	151.55	140.15	128.80	117.40	106.05	94.65	83.25	71.90
1648	1664	231.85	172.00	166.30	154.95	143.55	132.20	120.80	109.45	98.05	86.65	75.30
1664	1680	235.25	175.40	169.70	158.35	146.95	135.60	124.20	112.85	101.45	90.05	78.70
1680	1696	238.65	178.80	173.10	161.75	150.35	139.00	127.60	116.25	104.85	93.50	82.10
1696	1712	242.05	182.20	176.50	165.15	153.75	142.40	131.00	119.65	108.25	96.90	85.50
1712	1728	245.45	185.60	179.90	168.55	157.15	145.80	134.40	123.05	111.65	100.30	88.90
1728	1744	248.85	189.00	183.30	171.95	160.55	149.20	137.80	126.45	115.05	103.70	92.30
1744	1760	252.25	192.40	186.70	175.35	163.95	152.60	141.20	129.85	118.45	107.10	95.70
1760	1776	255.65	195.80	190.10	178.75	167.35	156.00	144.60	133.25	121.85	110.50	99.10
1776	1792	259.10	199.25	193.55	182.15	170.80	159.40	148.05	136.65	125.30	113.90	102.55
1792	1808	262.60	202.75	197.05	185.70	174.30	162.95	151.55	140.20	128.80	117.45	106.05
1808	1824	266.15	206.25	200.60	189.20	177.85	166.45	155.10	143.70	132.30	120.95	109.55
1824	1840	269.65	209.80	204.10	192.75	181.35	169.95	158.60	147.20	135.85	124.45	113.10
1840	1856	273.15	213.30	207.65	196.25	184.85	173.50	162.10	150.75	139.35	128.00	116.60
1856	1872	276.70	216.85	211.15	199.75	188.40	177.00	165.65	154.25	142.90	131.50	120.15
1872	1888	280.20	220.35	214.65	203.30	191.90	180.55	169.15	157.80	146.40	135.05	123.65
1888	1904	283.75	223.85	218.20	206.80	195.45	184.05	172.70	161.30	149.90	138.55	127.15
1904	1920	287.25	227.40	221.70	210.35	198.95	187.55	176.20	164.80	153.45	142.05	130.70
1920	1936	290.75	230.90	225.25	213.85	202.45	191.10	179.70	168.35	156.95	145.60	134.20
1936	1952	294.30	234.45	228.75	217.35	206.00	194.60	183.25	171.85	160.50	149.10	137.75
1952	1968	297.80	237.95	232.25	220.90	209.50	198.15	186.75	175.40	164.00	152.65	141.25
1968	1984	301.35	241.45	235.80	224.40	213.05	201.65	190.30	178.90	167.50	156.15	144.75
1984	2000	304.85	245.00	239.30	227.95	216.55	205.15	193.80	182.40	171.05	159.65	148.30

Ontario provincial tax deductions
Effective April 1, 2009
Biweekly (26 pay periods a year)
Also look up the tax deductions
in the federal table

Retenues d'impôt provincial de l'Ontario
En vigueur le 1er avril 2009
Aux deux semaines (26 périodes de paie par année)
Cherchez aussi les retenues d'impôt
dans la table fédérale

Pay Rémunération		Provincial claim codes/Codes de demande provinciaux										
		0	1	2	3	4	5	6	7	8	9	10
From Less than De Moins de		Deduct from each pay Retenez sur chaque paie										
1155 - 1171		77.60	56.95	54.70	50.25	45.80	41.35	36.90	32.45	28.00	19.80	11.55
1171 - 1187		78.50	57.85	55.60	51.15	46.70	42.25	37.80	33.35	28.90	21.60	12.70
1187 - 1203		79.40	58.75	56.50	52.05	47.60	43.15	38.70	34.25	29.80	23.40	14.50
1203 - 1219		80.30	59.65	57.40	52.95	48.50	44.05	39.60	35.15	30.70	25.20	16.30
1219 - 1235		81.20	60.55	58.35	53.85	49.40	44.95	40.50	36.05	31.60	27.00	18.10
1235 - 1251		82.10	61.45	59.25	54.80	50.35	45.85	41.40	36.95	32.50	28.05	19.95
1251 - 1267		83.00	62.35	60.15	55.70	51.25	46.80	42.35	37.90	33.40	28.95	21.75
1267 - 1283		83.95	63.25	61.05	56.60	52.15	47.70	43.25	38.80	34.35	29.90	23.55
1283 - 1299		84.85	64.15	61.95	57.50	53.05	48.60	44.15	39.70	35.25	30.80	25.35
1299 - 1315		85.75	65.05	62.85	58.40	53.95	49.50	45.05	40.60	36.15	31.70	27.15
1315 - 1331		86.65	65.95	63.75	59.30	54.85	50.40	45.95	41.50	37.05	32.60	28.15
1331 - 1347		87.55	66.85	64.65	60.20	55.75	51.30	46.85	42.40	37.95	33.50	29.05
1347 - 1363		88.45	67.80	65.55	61.10	56.65	52.20	47.75	43.30	38.85	34.40	29.95
1363 - 1379		89.35	68.70	66.45	62.00	57.55	53.10	48.65	44.20	39.75	35.30	30.85
1379 - 1395		90.40	69.75	67.50	63.05	58.60	54.15	49.70	45.25	40.80	36.35	31.90
1395 - 1411		92.25	71.60	69.35	64.90	60.45	56.00	51.55	47.10	42.65	38.20	33.75
1411 - 1427		94.20	73.50	71.30	66.85	62.40	57.95	53.50	49.05	44.60	40.15	35.70
1427 - 1443		96.55	75.90	73.65	69.20	64.75	60.30	55.85	51.40	46.95	42.50	38.05
1443 - 1459		98.90	78.25	76.00	71.55	67.10	62.65	58.20	53.75	49.30	44.85	40.40
1459 - 1475		101.25	80.60	78.35	73.90	69.45	65.00	60.55	56.10	51.65	47.20	42.75
1475 - 1491		103.50	82.80	80.60	76.15	71.70	67.25	62.80	58.35	53.90	49.45	45.00
1491 - 1507		104.90	84.20	82.00	77.55	73.10	68.65	64.20	59.75	55.30	50.85	46.40
1507 - 1523		106.30	85.60	83.40	78.95	74.50	70.05	65.60	61.15	56.70	52.25	47.80
1523 - 1539		107.70	87.00	84.80	80.35	75.90	71.45	67.00	62.55	58.10	53.65	49.20
1539 - 1555		109.10	88.40	86.20	81.75	77.30	72.85	68.40	63.95	59.50	55.05	50.60
1555 - 1571		110.50	89.80	87.60	83.15	78.70	74.25	69.80	65.35	60.90	56.45	52.00
1571 - 1587		111.90	91.20	89.00	84.55	80.10	75.65	71.20	66.75	62.30	57.85	53.40
1587 - 1603		113.30	92.60	90.40	85.95	81.50	77.05	72.60	68.15	63.70	59.25	54.80
1603 - 1619		114.70	94.00	91.80	87.35	82.90	78.45	74.00	69.55	65.10	60.65	56.20
1619 - 1635		116.10	95.40	93.20	88.75	84.30	79.85	75.40	70.95	66.50	62.05	57.60
1635 - 1651		117.50	96.85	94.60	90.15	85.70	81.25	76.80	72.35	67.90	63.45	59.00
1651 - 1667		118.90	98.25	96.00	91.55	87.10	82.65	78.20	73.75	69.30	64.85	60.40
1667 - 1683		120.35	99.65	97.45	93.00	88.55	84.10	79.65	75.20	70.75	66.30	61.85
1683 - 1699		121.75	101.10	98.85	94.40	89.95	85.50	81.05	76.60	72.15	67.70	63.25
1699 - 1715		123.15	102.50	100.25	95.80	91.35	86.90	82.45	78.00	73.55	69.10	64.65
1715 - 1731		124.60	103.90	101.70	97.25	92.80	88.35	83.90	79.45	75.00	70.55	66.10
1731 - 1747		126.00	105.35	103.10	98.65	94.20	89.75	85.30	80.85	76.40	71.95	67.50
1747 - 1763		127.40	106.75	104.50	100.05	95.60	91.15	86.70	82.25	77.80	73.35	68.90
1763 - 1779		128.85	108.15	105.95	101.50	97.05	92.60	88.15	83.70	79.25	74.80	70.35
1779 - 1795		130.25	109.60	107.35	102.90	98.45	94.00	89.55	85.10	80.65	76.20	71.75
1795 - 1811		131.75	111.05	108.85	104.40	99.95	95.50	91.05	86.60	82.15	77.70	73.20
1811 - 1827		133.20	112.55	110.30	105.85	101.40	96.95	92.50	88.05	83.60	79.15	74.70
1827 - 1843		134.65	114.00	111.75	107.30	102.85	98.40	93.95	89.50	85.05	80.60	76.15
1843 - 1859		137.35	116.65	114.45	110.00	105.55	101.10	96.65	92.20	87.75	83.30	78.85
1859 - 1875		142.80	122.15	119.90	115.45	111.00	106.55	102.10	97.65	93.20	88.75	84.30
1875 - 1891		144.80	124.15	121.90	117.45	113.00	108.55	104.10	99.65	95.20	90.75	86.30
1891 - 1907		146.30	125.60	123.40	118.95	114.50	110.05	105.60	101.15	96.70	92.25	87.80
1907 - 1923		147.75	127.10	124.85	120.40	115.95	111.50	107.05	102.60	98.15	93.70	89.25
1923 - 1939		149.20	128.55	126.30	121.85	117.40	112.95	108.50	104.05	99.60	95.15	90.70
1939 - 1955		150.65	130.00	127.80	123.35	118.90	114.45	110.00	105.50	101.05	96.60	92.15
1955 - 1971		152.15	131.45	129.25	124.80	120.35	115.90	111.45	107.00	102.55	98.10	93.65
1971 - 1987		153.60	132.95	130.70	126.25	121.80	117.35	112.90	108.45	104.00	99.55	95.10
1987 - 2003		155.05	134.40	132.15	127.70	123.25	118.80	114.35	109.90	105.45	101.00	96.55
2003 - 2019		156.55	135.85	133.65	129.20	124.75	120.30	115.85	111.40	106.95	102.50	98.05
2019 - 2035		158.00	137.35	135.10	130.65	126.20	121.75	117.30	112.85	108.40	103.95	99.50

This table is available on TOD   E-9   Vous pouvez obtenir cette table sur TSD

Canada Pension Plan Contributions
Biweekly (26 pay periods a year)

Cotisations au Régime de pensions du Canada
Aux deux semaines (26 périodes de paie par année)

Pay Rémunération		CPP RPC	Pay Rémunération		CPP RPC	Pay Rémunération		CPP RPC	Pay Rémunération		CPP RPC
From - De	To - À		From - De	To - À		From - De	To - À		From - De	To - À	
1763.60	1763.80	80.64	1778.15	1778.34	81.36	2370.78	2380.77	110.94	3090.78	3100.77	146.58
1763.81	1764.00	80.65	1778.35	1778.54	81.37	2380.78	2390.77	111.43	3100.78	3110.77	147.07
1764.01	1764.20	80.66	1778.55	1778.75	81.38	2390.78	2400.77	111.93	3110.78	3120.77	147.57
1764.21	1764.40	80.67	1778.76	1778.95	81.39	2400.78	2410.77	112.42	3120.78	3130.77	148.06
1764.41	1764.60	80.68	1778.96	1779.15	81.40	2410.78	2420.77	112.92	3130.78	3140.77	148.56
1764.61	1764.81	80.69	1779.16	1779.35	81.41	2420.78	2430.77	113.41	3140.78	3150.77	149.05
1764.82	1765.01	80.70	1779.36	1779.55	81.42	2430.78	2440.77	113.91	3150.78	3160.77	149.55
1765.02	1765.21	80.71	1779.56	1779.76	81.43	2440.78	2450.77	114.40	3160.78	3170.77	150.04
1765.22	1765.41	80.72	1779.77	1779.96	81.44	2450.78	2460.77	114.90	3170.78	3180.77	150.54
1765.42	1765.62	80.73	1779.97	1780.16	81.45	2460.78	2470.77	115.39	3180.78	3190.77	151.03
1765.63	1765.82	80.74	1780.17	1780.36	81.46	2470.78	2480.77	115.89	3190.78	3200.77	151.53
1765.83	1766.02	80.75	1780.37	1780.56	81.47	2480.78	2490.77	116.38	3200.78	3210.77	152.02
1766.03	1766.22	80.76	1780.57	1780.77	81.48	2490.78	2500.77	116.88	3210.78	3220.77	152.52
1766.23	1766.42	80.77	1780.78	1790.77	81.73	2500.78	2510.77	117.37	3220.78	3230.77	153.01
1766.43	1766.63	80.78	1790.78	1800.77	82.23	2510.78	2520.77	117.87	3230.78	3240.77	153.51
1766.64	1766.83	80.79	1800.78	1810.77	82.72	2520.78	2530.77	118.36	3240.78	3250.77	154.00
1766.84	1767.03	80.80	1810.78	1820.77	83.22	2530.78	2540.77	118.86	3250.78	3260.77	154.50
1767.04	1767.23	80.81	1820.78	1830.77	83.71	2540.78	2550.77	119.35	3260.78	3270.77	154.99
1767.24	1767.43	80.82	1830.78	1840.77	84.21	2550.78	2560.77	119.85	3270.78	3280.77	155.49
1767.44	1767.64	80.83	1840.78	1850.77	84.70	2560.78	2570.77	120.34	3280.78	3290.77	155.98
1767.65	1767.84	80.84	1850.78	1860.77	85.20	2570.78	2580.77	120.84	3290.78	3300.77	156.48
1767.85	1768.04	80.85	1860.78	1870.77	85.69	2580.78	2590.77	121.33	3300.78	3310.77	156.97
1768.05	1768.24	80.86	1870.78	1880.77	86.19	2590.78	2600.77	121.83	3310.78	3320.77	157.47
1768.25	1768.44	80.87	1880.78	1890.77	86.68	2600.78	2610.77	122.32	3320.78	3330.77	157.96
1768.45	1768.65	80.88	1890.78	1900.77	87.18	2610.78	2620.77	122.82	3330.78	3340.77	158.46
1768.66	1768.85	80.89	1900.78	1910.77	87.67	2620.78	2630.77	123.31	3340.78	3350.77	158.95
1768.86	1769.05	80.90	1910.78	1920.77	88.17	2630.78	2640.77	123.81	3350.78	3360.77	159.45
1769.06	1769.25	80.91	1920.78	1930.77	88.66	2640.78	2650.77	124.30	3360.78	3370.77	159.94
1769.26	1769.45	80.92	1930.78	1940.77	89.16	2650.78	2660.77	124.80	3370.78	3380.77	160.44
1769.46	1769.66	80.93	1940.78	1950.77	89.65	2660.78	2670.77	125.29	3380.78	3390.77	160.93
1769.67	1769.86	80.94	1950.78	1960.77	90.15	2670.78	2680.77	125.79	3390.78	3400.77	161.43
1769.87	1770.06	80.95	1960.78	1970.77	90.64	2680.78	2690.77	126.28	3400.78	3410.77	161.92
1770.07	1770.26	80.96	1970.78	1980.77	91.14	2690.78	2700.77	126.78	3410.78	3420.77	162.42
1770.27	1770.46	80.97	1980.78	1990.77	91.63	2700.78	2710.77	127.27	3420.78	3430.77	162.91
1770.47	1770.67	80.98	1990.78	2000.77	92.13	2710.78	2720.77	127.77	3430.78	3440.77	163.41
1770.68	1770.87	80.99	2000.78	2010.77	92.62	2720.78	2730.77	128.26	3440.78	3450.77	163.90
1770.88	1771.07	81.00	2010.78	2020.77	93.12	2730.78	2740.77	128.76	3450.78	3460.77	164.40
1771.08	1771.27	81.01	2020.78	2030.77	93.61	2740.78	2750.77	129.25	3460.78	3470.77	164.89
1771.28	1771.47	81.02	2030.78	2040.77	94.11	2750.78	2760.77	129.75	3470.78	3480.77	165.39
1771.48	1771.68	81.03	2040.78	2050.77	94.60	2760.78	2770.77	130.24	3480.78	3490.77	165.88
1771.69	1771.88	81.04	2050.78	2060.77	95.10	2770.78	2780.77	130.74	3490.78	3500.77	166.38
1771.89	1772.08	81.05	2060.78	2070.77	95.59	2780.78	2790.77	131.23	3500.78	3510.77	166.87
1772.09	1772.28	81.06	2070.78	2080.77	96.09	2790.78	2800.77	131.73	3510.78	3520.77	167.37
1772.29	1772.48	81.07	2080.78	2090.77	96.58	2800.78	2810.77	132.22	3520.78	3530.77	167.86
1772.49	1772.69	81.08	2090.78	2100.77	97.08	2810.78	2820.77	132.72	3530.78	3540.77	168.36
1772.70	1772.89	81.09	2100.78	2110.77	97.57	2820.78	2830.77	133.21	3540.78	3550.77	168.85
1772.90	1773.09	81.10	2110.78	2120.77	98.07	2830.78	2840.77	133.71	3550.78	3560.77	169.35
1773.10	1773.29	81.11	2120.78	2130.77	98.56	2840.78	2850.77	134.20	3560.78	3570.77	169.84
1773.30	1773.49	81.12	2130.78	2140.77	99.06	2850.78	2860.77	134.70	3570.78	3580.77	170.34
1773.50	1773.70	81.13	2140.78	2150.77	99.55	2860.78	2870.77	135.19	3580.78	3590.77	170.83
1773.71	1773.90	81.14	2150.78	2160.77	100.05	2870.78	2880.77	135.69	3590.78	3600.77	171.33
1773.91	1774.10	81.15	2160.78	2170.77	100.54	2880.78	2890.77	136.18	3600.78	3610.77	171.82
1774.11	1774.30	81.16	2170.78	2180.77	101.04	2890.78	2900.77	136.68	3610.78	3620.77	172.32
1774.31	1774.50	81.17	2180.78	2190.77	101.53	2900.78	2910.77	137.17	3620.78	3630.77	172.81
1774.51	1774.71	81.18	2190.78	2200.77	102.03	2910.78	2920.77	137.67	3630.78	3640.77	173.31
1774.72	1774.91	81.19	2200.78	2210.77	102.52	2920.78	2930.77	138.16	3640.78	3650.77	173.80
1774.92	1775.11	81.20	2210.78	2220.77	103.02	2930.78	2940.77	138.66	3650.78	3660.77	174.30
1775.12	1775.31	81.21	2220.78	2230.77	103.51	2940.78	2950.77	139.15	3660.78	3670.77	174.79
1775.32	1775.51	81.22	2230.78	2240.77	104.01	2950.78	2960.77	139.65	3670.78	3680.77	175.29
1775.52	1775.72	81.23	2240.78	2250.77	104.50	2960.78	2970.77	140.14	3680.78	3690.77	175.78
1775.73	1775.92	81.24	2250.78	2260.77	105.00	2970.78	2980.77	140.64	3690.78	3700.77	176.28
1775.93	1776.12	81.25	2260.78	2270.77	105.49	2980.78	2990.77	141.13	3700.78	3710.77	176.77
1776.13	1776.32	81.26	2270.78	2280.77	105.99	2990.78	3000.77	141.63	3710.78	3720.77	177.27
1776.33	1776.52	81.27	2280.78	2290.77	106.48	3000.78	3010.77	142.12	3720.78	3730.77	177.76
1776.53	1776.73	81.28	2290.78	2300.77	106.98	3010.78	3020.77	142.62	3730.78	3740.77	178.26
1776.74	1776.93	81.29	2300.78	2310.77	107.47	3020.78	3030.77	143.11	3740.78	3750.77	178.75
1776.94	1777.13	81.30	2310.78	2320.77	107.97	3030.78	3040.77	143.61	3750.78	3760.77	179.25
1777.14	1777.33	81.31	2320.78	2330.77	108.46	3040.78	3050.77	144.10	3760.78	3770.77	179.74
1777.34	1777.53	81.32	2330.78	2340.77	108.96	3050.78	3060.77	144.60	3770.78	3780.77	180.24
1777.54	1777.74	81.33	2340.78	2350.77	109.45	3060.78	3070.77	145.09	3780.78	3790.77	180.73
1777.75	1777.94	81.34	2350.78	2360.77	109.95	3070.78	3080.77	145.59	3790.78	3800.77	181.23
1777.95	1778.14	81.35	2360.78	2370.77	110.44	3080.78	3090.77	146.08	3800.78	3810.77	181.72

Employee's maximum CPP contribution for the year 2009 is $2,118.60   B-45   La cotisation maximale de l'employé au RPC pour l'année 2009 est de 2 118,60 $

Payroll tables and excerpts from the Canada Revenue Agency website reproduced with permission of the Minister of Public Works and Government Services Canada, 2010.